THE REST
I WILL
KILL

ALSO BY BRIAN McGINTY

Lincoln's Greatest Case:
The River, the Bridge, and the Making of America

Lincoln and the Court

The Body of John Merryman:
Abraham Lincoln and the Suspension of Habeas Corpus

John Brown's Trial

Strong Wine: The Life and Legend of Agoston Haraszthy

The Oatman Massacre:
A Tale of Desert Captivity and Survival

Paderewski at Paso Robles:
A Great Pianist's Home Away from Home in California

A Toast to Eclipse:
Arpad Haraszthy and the Sparkling Wine of Old San Francisco

The Palace Inns:
A Connoisseur's Guide to Historic American Hotels

Haraszthy at the Mint
(Famous California Trials Series)

We the People:
A Special Issue Commemorating the Two-Hundredth Anniversary of
the U.S. Constitution (American History Illustrated)

THE REST
I WILL
KILL

WILLIAM TILLMAN

AND THE UNFORGETTABLE STORY OF
HOW A FREE BLACK MAN
REFUSED TO BECOME A SLAVE

BRIAN McGINTY

LIVERIGHT PUBLISHING CORPORATION

A Division of W. W. Norton & Company

Independent Publishers Since 1923

New York · London

3 1489 00690 5648

Copyright © 2016 by Brian McGinty

All rights reserved
Printed in the United States of America
First Edition

For information about permission to reproduce selections from this book,
write to Permissions, Liveright Publishing Corporation,
a division of W. W. Norton & Company, Inc.,
500 Fifth Avenue, New York, NY 10110

For information about special discounts for bulk purchases, please contact
W. W. Norton Special Sales at specialsales@wwnorton.com or 800-233-4830

Manufacturing by Berryville Graphics
Book design by Chris Welch Design
Production manager: Julia Druskin

Library of Congress Cataloging-in-Publication Data

Names: McGinty, Brian, author.
Title: The rest I will kill : William Tillman and the unforgettable story of
how a free black man refused to become a slave / Brian McGinty.
Description: First edition. | New York : Liveright Publishing Corporation,
2016. | Includes bibliographical references and index.
Identifiers: LCCN 2016014687 | ISBN 9781631491290 (hardcover)
Subjects: LCSH: Tilghman, Billy. | United States—History—Civil War,
1861–1865—Participation, African American. | United
States—History—Civil War, 1861–1865—Naval operations. | Free African
Americans—Biography. | S.J. Waring (Schooner)
Classification: LCC E540.N3 M238 2016 | DDC 973.7/415—dc23 LC record
available at http://lccn.loc.gov/2016014687

Liveright Publishing Corporation
500 Fifth Avenue, New York, N.Y. 10110
www.wwnorton.com

W. W. Norton & Company Ltd.
Castle House, 75/76 Wells Street, London W1T 3QT

1 2 3 4 5 6 7 8 9 0

TO THE MEMORY OF ABRAHAM LINCOLN,

ATTORNEY-AT-LAW

CONTENTS

The story told in this book is true. It is history, not fiction. It is an account of events that actually took place, of words that were actually spoken, of blood that was actually spilled, and of freedom that was actually preserved on a fateful voyage at sea.

THE REST
I WILL
KILL

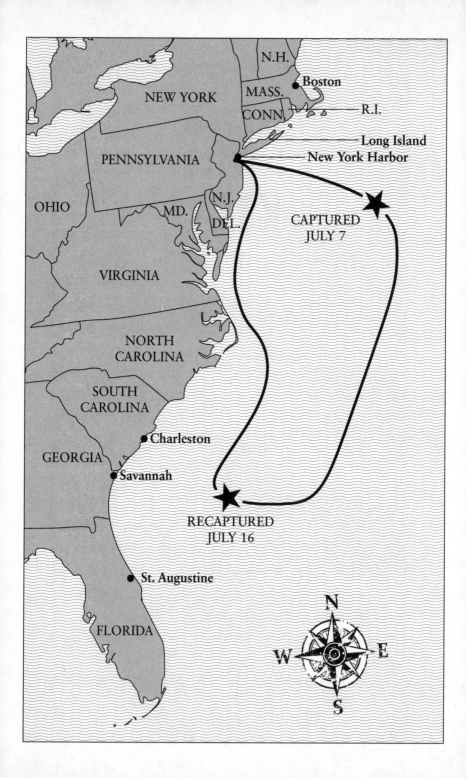

PROLOGUE

Early in the afternoon of Sunday, July 21, 1861, the merchant schooner *S. J. Waring* passed through the Narrows, which guard the entrance to New York Harbor, and sailed toward the Battery at the foot of Manhattan Island. A harbor pilot had come aboard to guide the vessel safely into port, but the man in real command was a twenty-seven-year-old free black man from Rhode Island named William Tillman. Young, strong, and determined, Tillman had left New York only seventeen days earlier as the *Waring*'s cook and steward on a commercial voyage that was to have taken it to Montevideo, Uruguay, and Buenos Aires, Argentina. But the voyage was interrupted only four days out of New York when the vessel was stopped at sea and boarded by privateers from the Confederate States of America. Declaring the schooner a prize of the war then being fought between the North and the South, the privateers had taken command of the vessel and pointed it toward an unnamed secessionist port where it would be condemned, and Tillman, the only black man aboard, would be hauled in irons to a public auction and sold into slavery. Determined not to surrender his freedom to that fate, Tillman had recaptured the *Waring* when it was less than one day's sail from Charleston, South Carolina, and, defying the many dangers posed by the war-torn sea-lanes then separating the schooner from New York, directed the vessel and its remaining crew back to the North.

Preliminary reports of the *Waring*'s misfortune at sea, picked up by other seagoing vessels, had leaked into New York, but the facts surrounding its return north were not known until Monday morning, when Tillman and the other men aboard came ashore and were questioned by the harbor police and newspaper reporters. The full story of his recapture of the schooner then became public—a story that astounded New Yorkers and excited newspaper readers throughout the country.

Tillman's story commanded attention both because of the bravery he had demonstrated at sea and because of the unprecedented crisis in which the United States then found itself. Fort Sumter in the harbor of Charleston, South Carolina, had surrendered to Confederate artillery bombardment only three months earlier. On the same day that Tillman sailed the *Waring* back into New York Harbor, Union and Confederate armies had met in their first major encounter, the battle that would become known in the North as Bull Run (later called First Bull Run) and in the South as Manassas (later First Manassas). Confused and badly disoriented, the Union soldiers had fled the field of that conflict in humiliating disarray.

In bold contrast, Tillman had rescued the *Waring* from its Southern captors. He had triumphed over the secessionists who sought to disrupt Northern shipping with their privateer vessels (some called them "pirate" vessels, although Confederate sympathizers vigorously disputed the description). The black man was surrounded by enthusiastic crowds as he was taken to the headquarters of the harbor police, then to the offices of the United States marshal and district attorney, and then onto the stage of the premier entertainment venue in New York, P. T. Barnum's American Museum on lower Broadway. Currier & Ives published a lithographic portrait of him that was used to advertise his appearances at Barnum's and helped to spread his fame beyond New York. He filed a claim in U.S. District Court for what the admiralty law calls "salvage"—a monetary reward long guaranteed in English and American law for those who save imperiled vessels at sea—and, after a spirited trial, the judge awarded him a handsome sum and warmly endorsed his maritime heroism. The North needed a hero, and Tillman filled the bill.

But the public's focus soon changed, and Tillman's story fell into a long and in some ways understandable neglect. The nation sank deeper and deeper into a turbulent maelstrom of war and destruction. Larger and larger armies from all sections of the country were sent into increasingly bloody encounters. Casualties in frightening numbers were suffered on both sides of the conflict.

People in both the North and the South understood that the war was on at least one level about the institution of slavery as it was then practiced in the United States—and had been for nearly three centuries past.[1] Just under four million men, women, and children were held in bondage below the Mason-Dixon Line because they did not belong to the same race as the men who called themselves their masters. Strong, healthy black men, women, and children commanded good prices in the Southern slave markets that dotted the land from Maryland and Virginia in the Northeast as far as Arkansas, Louisiana, and Texas in the Southwest. There was a market in slaves—much like the markets for land or stocks or bonds—that was a good source of profits for white men who knew when to buy and when to sell, when to take advantage of fluctuations in price, when to go to the market, and when to hold back. And the number of slaves was growing each year. Although the importation of slaves into the United States had been forbidden by federal law since 1808,[2] smugglers still managed to bring some in via Caribbean islands, to show them in the slave markets, and to reap the profits their illegal trading produced.[3]

But not all the African Americans in the United States on the eve of the Civil War were slaves. There were, according to the census records, about half a million free blacks, many of whom lived in the North.[4] There they were not burdened with legally enforced bondage, although they were denied most of the rights and privileges that white Americans enjoyed: the right to vote, to freely buy and sell land, to sit on juries, to patronize white-owned hotels and restaurants, and, perhaps most important, to attend schools with whites. Where schools existed, they were almost uniformly segregated, and the number of public schools that were open to African Americans was pitifully small.

William Tillman was one of the free blacks who lived in the North. For four years he had been employed as a cook and steward by Jonas Smith & Co., the Long Island–based owner of the *S. J. Waring*.[5] He valued the employment, for it was better than the plight of so many other African Americans who had even more menial jobs—or none at all. But it did not offer any real chance of advancement. The United States was widely praised as a land of opportunity, a country in which men could rise from a lowly status to one of respect and even admiration. But the opportunities available to white men were almost completely denied to blacks. And the basic means of taking advantage of those opportunities were closed to African Americans because they were denied educations. They were not taught to read or write. And without these fundamental skills even self-improvement was unavailable to them. And so, after his act of Civil War heroism was completed, William Tillman retreated—like millions of his fellow African Americans— into the shadows in which he had lived before the war. He slipped out of the public eye and was soon forgotten. The war continued to rage, but he was no longer its hero.

The Civil War was in large part a struggle on land between opposing armies. Much of the conflict, however, took place at sea and on navigable waterways after Confederate president Jefferson Davis commissioned privateers to capture Northern ships and Union president Abraham Lincoln declared a blockade of the Southern coast. Tillman found himself in the middle of this struggle when he left New York aboard the *Waring*.

The commissioning of Southern privateers, like the blockade of the Confederate coast, raised troubling issues that lay at the heart of secession and the resulting war. Was secession constitutional? Did the Confederate States of America acquire true independence and national sovereignty as a result of their secession? Or was their action nothing more than rebellion and treason? These issues sharply divided Lincoln and Davis and had profound repercussions in the maritime combat of the war. They were litigated in two trials that took place in Philadelphia and New York at about the same time that William Tillman's trial was heard in New York, and the trials produced dramatically different results, with captured privateers in Philadelphia being convicted of piracy and sentenced to death and privateers in New York escaping punishment as the result of a hung jury. Tillman's story must be told against the background of these fundamental issues, for they impinged on the legality of what he did. Were the privateers who captured the *Waring* criminal pirates? Was Tillman justified in rising up against them and recapturing the schooner? Or were they the duly constituted representatives of a sovereign foreign nation and as such, people whom Tillman was obligated to obey?

The story told in this book centers on the bravery of William Tillman, the emotional torture he suffered when the Confederates threatened to enslave him, and the perils he overcame in bringing himself and the *S. J. Waring* back to New York from their Southern captivity. But it is not his story alone, for millions of other black Americans—some born free like Tillman, others born into bondage—suffered similar oppression and indignity in the nineteenth century. Many displayed courage and valor similar to Tillman's during the war and were similarly forgotten after the fighting concluded. I have made serious efforts to discover the facts of Tillman's life after he was acclaimed as a hero in the early days of the Civil War. Beyond a few bits of fragmentary information, and a lot of speculation, however, the story of the life he led in later years has all but disappeared.[6] He has become a cipher, a dimly remembered footnote to a tumultuous chapter in America's past, one of millions who were shunted aside, hidden, and forgotten.

But Tillman should not remain a forgotten hero, for the perils he faced aboard the *S. J. Waring* were genuine; the bravery he displayed in rescuing himself and the schooner from those perils was equally so; and the acclaim showered on him when he brought the *Waring* back to New York helped, if only briefly, to buoy Union hopes for eventual victory in the conflict then raging between the North and the South.

ONE

A FREE BLACK MAN

William Tillman was born in Milford, Delaware, about 1834.[1] His parents were free blacks and, as such, members of a small but significant colony of free African Americans in a state that sanctioned slavery. Delaware was the most northerly state whose laws still authorized human bondage in 1861, although the number of slaves there was small, and growing smaller each year.

African Americans had lived in the area that was later to become the United States for nearly three hundred years before Tillman was born. Some had come to Florida in the sixteenth century with French and Spanish colonists, some to the New Netherlands (later New York) with Dutch mercantilists in the seventeenth century, yet others to Virginia with English settlers in the seventeenth and eighteenth centuries.[2] Swedes were the first Europeans to settle the area later called Delaware, which they called New Sweden. Their occupation, however, was short, for in 1655 the Swedes were ousted by the Dutch, who were in turn ousted by the English only ten years later.[3]

The first African American to arrive in Delaware was a

man named Anthony (often called "Black Anthony" in histories of Delaware), who was brought there by Swedish colonists in 1639.[4] Though little is known of Anthony, the scanty record shows that he worked for one of the governors of New Sweden and eventually purchased some goods for himself, perhaps because he had by that time become a free man.[5] Many thousands of African slaves were brought to Delaware after Anthony, some by the Swedes but most by the Dutch. The agriculture the Dutch introduced into the area required laborers to till the land, plant and harvest the crops, and load them onto ships for transport to nearby colonies, the Caribbean, or Brazil. Since the Dutch themselves were unwilling to perform the necessary agricultural labor, they procured Africans to do the work, and slavery soon became a booming industry and an integral part of the colony's social and economic life.[6]

Most of the slaves came to Delaware on slave-trading ships that sailed from the west coast of Africa to the Atlantic Seaboard, while others may originally have been free men and women who were made slaves only after they set foot in Delaware. Many came from the Eastern Shore of Maryland, a richly productive agricultural area that abutted Delaware on the west and south, while others were brought north from Virginia, which occupied the southern end of the Delmarva Peninsula below Maryland and Delaware. Evidence suggests that a number of slaves were brought by boat from the Carolinas and even more from New York, where slavery persisted through the first quarter of the nineteenth century.[7]

Although there were many farms in Delaware, a plantation economy on the scale of Virginia and the Carolinas never developed there. Tobacco was the first profitable crop, but it quickly depleted the soil and prompted colonists to replace it with corn and wheat.[8] Slaves constituted an estimated 20 percent of the population of Delaware when the English took over in 1664, but by 1790, when the first U.S. Census was taken, they were only 15 percent, while free blacks were 7 percent.[9] As a result Delaware in 1790 had the largest percentage of free blacks of any state in the Union, with Maryland and Virginia having only 2 percent each and Pennsylvania and New York just 1 percent.[10]

The road to freedom for a slave in Delaware was often long and tortuous. A few of the state's free blacks may have achieved their free status in Northern states and kept it after they relocated to Delaware to find employment, while others were able to purchase their freedom from owners who had lost confidence in the economic viability of slavery and preferred to invest their capital more productively.[11] Since the growing season in Delaware was short, consisting mostly of the warm months of June, July, and August, farmers could save a lot of money by hiring free laborers to work for only three months of the year instead of having to support slaves the year round.[12] Most slaves, however, achieved their free status through formal documents signed by their owners (called manumissions), either during their owners' lifetimes or by testament upon their deaths.[13]

Fully aware of the system's brutality, whites in Delaware rarely questioned its morality during the colonial period. Like slaveholders in other colonies, they regarded the institution as a settled part of their economic and social structure. Beginning in the Revolutionary period, however, they began to express some doubts about the institution. The Enlightenment, which had done so much to inspire the war for independence from Great Britain, was in part responsible for the change in thinking. If, as the Declaration of Independence declared, "all men are endowed by their Creator with certain unalienable rights," and if these include the right to "life, liberty and the pursuit of happiness," what justification could there be for consigning some men to the degradation of chattel slavery?

Religious thinking about slavery was also evolving. Most of the traditional churches had not questioned the morality of the institution, but some newer disciplines were beginning to condemn it. The Society of Friends (Quakers) was one of the first to question the morality of slavery, although many Quakers had in fact owned slaves in the early colonial years; and the Methodist Church began in the late eighteenth century to preach that slavery was morally wrong. (In the early part of the nineteenth century, however, Methodism would lose its antislavery fervor and defend it in many Southern states).[14] For all these reasons, and perhaps others (some economic, some undoubtedly political), the number of slaves in Delaware declined dramatically in the early years of the Republic, with 6,153 in 1800 and only 1,798 in 1860. During the same period the numbers of free blacks increased from 8,268 in 1800 to 19,829 in 1860.[15]

Beginning in the 1790s, there were periodic efforts to end

all slavery in Delaware. An attempt to include emancipation in the state constitution adopted in 1792 was unsuccessful. In 1803 a bill introduced in the state legislature to abolish slavery on a gradual basis failed by one vote. And in 1847, another bill to gradually abolish slavery failed by one vote in the state Senate.[16]

While slavery was declining in Delaware, it was also under siege in other, more northern states. Slavery had been practiced in all the North American colonies at early dates, but a concerted movement to emancipate slaves began in Vermont in 1771, continued in Massachusetts and Pennsylvania in the 1780s, and reached four other Northern states by 1804.[17] New York did not abolish the institution until 1827, Connecticut not until 1848, and a form of involuntary servitude survived in New Jersey right up to the Civil War.[18] While slavery was under attack in Northern states, it seemed to be growing weaker and weaker in Delaware. Some in fact thought it was on the verge of dying.[19] Yet the powers that be were stubbornly resistant to proclaiming its death.

As early as 1787, when the Constitution was drafted in Philadelphia, it became clear that the United States would be divided between "free" states in the North and "slave" states in the South, for the national charter included key provisions whose sole purpose was to win support from Southern slave-holders.[20] Delaware was in the South (although not in the Deep South), and its sympathy for the institution that was growing larger and more powerful with each passing year in Virginia, the Carolinas, Georgia, and the newer slave states to the west—Alabama, Mississippi, Louisiana, Arkansas, Missouri, and Texas—was persistent.

Why then was slavery abolished in the Northern but not the Southern states? It has been argued by some that the soil and climate in the Northern states were not suitable for the kind of large-scale farming that made slave labor so profitable farther south. If they had been, Northerners would have been as strongly attached to slavery as Southerners, for they were every bit as fond of making money—regardless of the moral cost—as their Southern brethren.[21] But this explanation has been challenged on the grounds that slaves had in fact been profitably employed on the small farms of the North before abolition began, and they could have been employed just as well thereafter. Further, slave labor was well adapted to the kind of manufacturing and commercial enterprises that increasingly characterized the North. The religious scruples of some Northerners accounted in part for the movement to end slavery in that part of the country, but so did the growing realization of many Northerners that it was hypocritical to deny freedom to one group of men while championing it for themselves. As the historian David Brion Davis has written, slavery "did not decline or disappear in the North because it was uneconomical, unproductive, or a burden on the economy."[22] It ended because of ideas rooted in religion and the ideals of the Enlightenment.

Southerners recognized the same truths as Northerners (the Declaration of Independence had, after all, been drafted by Thomas Jefferson, one of the most prominent of all the

Southerners), but as time passed and Southern agriculture expanded farther into the South and the West—and as the production of cotton with cheap slave labor became more and more profitable—Southerners seemed to forget the ideals of the Revolution and developed elaborate justifications for the continuation of what they called "the peculiar institution."[23] In Delaware in the middle of the nineteenth century the thinking seemed to be divided, with a substantial part of the local population sharing the belief that slavery offended morality and justice while another realized that slavery was profitable and that it would be difficult to end it without upsetting the prosperity of the American South. A large number of whites also sympathized with Southern slaveholders and feared that free blacks would pose a danger to the white population.[24] The slave revolution in Haiti in the 1790s, and black uprisings and conspiracies in Southern states—one led by Gabriel Prosser in Virginia in 1800, another by Denmark Vesey in South Carolina in 1822, and a third by Nat Turner in Virginia in 1831—had convinced many whites that blacks would rise up in a bloody furor unless they were kept under rigid constraints.[25] And so Delaware was stalemated, watching silently as slavery seemed to dissolve but unable to declare a final end to it.

William Tillman and his parents were members of the growing population of free blacks in Delaware. Beyond that fact, however, the available historical record reveals next to nothing about them. We do not even know how they acquired the surname of Tillman—or Tilghman or Tilman, as the family name was sometimes spelled.

Africans who arrived in the Americas came with no surnames in the European sense, and for most of the time they lived in slavery only with personal names. Eventually, however, it was expected that they would adopt surnames. By 1800 it is estimated that almost all the free blacks in Delaware had done so, and that those names were then, in the European fashion, applied to all members of their families.[26]

The Tillman name was neither particularly common nor rare in Delaware. Census and marriage records for the state reveal a fair number of black men and women named Tillman, Tilghman, or Tilman, some of whom may have been members of the same family as William Tillman. A free black named Prince Tilghman, for example, was a tenant farmer in the late 1790s in Murderkill Hundred in Kent County, where official records showed that he owned twenty-three cattle, twenty-five sheep, eight pigs, and five horses, altogether a considerable personal estate for any farmer in those days.[27] The federal census for 1800 showed that the same Prince Tilghman was the head of a household of six persons.[28] Marriage records for Delaware show that he was licensed to marry one Sarah Jackson in October 1831.[29] An entry in the 1840 census indicates that Prince Tilghman was the head of a household of seven persons, one of whom was a free black male under the age of ten years.[30] (William Tillman was in that age group in 1840.) The 1850 census reveals that Prince Tilman (*sic*), then seventy-five years of age, was living with Sarah Tilman (*sic*), then fifty, in

Dover Hundred in Kent County.[31] The census also shows
that a family of blacks named Tilman (*sic*) was living in
Wilmington in New Castle County in 1850. This family was
headed by a seventy-year-old man named John and included
six children, one of whom was named William. This William
Tilman, however, was stated to be twenty-one years old.[32]
Because the William Tillman who was aboard the *S. J. Waring* in 1861 would have been sixteen years old in 1850, this
entry is almost certainly not for the same man. The absence
of verifiable records about William Tillman's life in Delaware is disappointing but not particularly surprising, for
many blacks lived lives of near anonymity throughout America in the years before the Civil War.

Although we have more information that reveals the kind of
lives free blacks lived in Delaware in the years leading up to
the great national conflict, it is almost wholly dismal and dis-
couraging. The antipathy, and in many cases fear, that whites
felt for African Americans was reflected in a web of legal and
social restrictions that made the lives of free blacks anything
but equal to those then lived by whites.

Much of that information comes from the research of a free
black man from Philadelphia who went into Delaware in 1837
to conduct a study and report his findings to the American
Anti-Slavery Society, of which he was an agent. William Yates
regarded Delaware as a critical ground in the struggle for the
abolition of slavery that was then being waged in most Northern states. He reported his findings in a letter to two abolition-

ist newspapers then published in New York.[33] Using figures
derived from the federal census, Yates determined that there
were only nine hundred slaveholders in Delaware and 56,701
residents who owned no slaves. "Under this view of the case,"
he wrote, "I had hoped to find slavery in Delaware merely
nominal." He found instead that the free blacks in the state
were "only *nominally* free." "Under the wretched and mongrel
system of laws which have been enacted in regard to them,"
he wrote, "they enjoy but a mongrel liberty, a mere mock freedom. They are truly neither slaves nor free; being subject to
many of the disabilities and disadvantages of both conditions,
and enjoying few of the benefits of either."[34]

The employment opportunities available to free blacks in
Delaware were not inviting. Most worked as farmhands or
domestic servants.[35] A few were able to become self-employed
farmers by acquiring land as purchasers or tenants.[36] As the
number of free blacks in Delaware increased, many moved
to cities and towns in hopes of finding better opportunities.
By the 1850s the greatest number of free blacks lived in and
around Wilmington in the northern end of the state or in
the more southern communities of Milford, Milton, Lewes,
Seaford, and Laurel.[37] Most women found work as domestic
servants or washerwomen, and most men became laborers.[38]
Some men, however, were able to work as waiters, cooks, gar-
deners, wagon and carriage drivers, or stable hands. A limited
number of jobs were also available in skilled trades such as
carpentry, masonry, blacksmithing, coopering, butchering,
weaving, and barbering.[39] But because the jobs available to

men in the urban centers were often of short duration, they frequently had to return to the farmlands and move from place to place looking for work.[40]

One inviting source of employment *was* available to free black men, however. This was on the ships and boats that plied the Delaware River and went out to sea loaded with the products of local farms. Maritime employment was not available to a large number of blacks, as the farms were not particularly large and the number of available jobs was relatively small, but it was an opportunity that many longed for. The railroad that connected Wilmington in the North with Virginia in the South was not completed until 1859, so the great bulk of cargo transportation in Delaware continued to be on water as the Civil War drew near.[41]

The poor employment opportunities in Delaware, coupled with the state's many restrictions on the freedom of blacks, persuaded more and more free blacks to leave the state in hope that they could find better lives elsewhere. Many slaves escaped their bondage with the aid of the Underground Railroad, while free blacks simply gathered up their possessions and headed north, first to Philadelphia, where slavery was prohibited by law, but also into New Jersey, New York, and beyond.[42]

If blacks were unhappy with their lives in Delaware, whites were no more pleased to have so many free blacks in their midst, and they took steps to encourage their exits. In 1849 the state legislature enacted a draconian law that made it illegal for free blacks in Delaware to be both unemployed and poor.

If the local justice of the peace concluded that a free black was guilty of violating the statute, he ordered the sheriff to sell the offender to a master for whom the black would work "in the capacity of a servant" until the next January 1. The master was authorized to enforce the black person's "obedience to lawful commands by moderate corrections and by suitable and sufficient means." The status of free blacks under this law was thus a near approximation of chattel slavery itself. To add to the misery it imposed on free blacks, the Delaware law gave the convicted men and women only thirty days after January 1 to find new employment. If they could not do this in the middle of the winter, when farm jobs were nearly nonexistent, they would be sentenced to another year of legally compelled labor and servitude.[43] The many restrictions to which free blacks were subjected in Delaware, combined with the cruel law of 1849, gave the state the reputation of what one historian has called "the least hospitable place in the Union for freedmen prior to the Civil War."[44]

Despite these and similar privations, we do not know why William Tillman and his family left Delaware. We know only that they did so about eleven years before William found himself aboard the *S. J. Waring* in July 1861. From this we can conclude that they made their break with the state in 1850.[45] The 1849 law imposing involuntary servitude on unemployed free blacks may well have contributed to their decision, although economic opportunities farther north may also have played a part.

If free blacks wanted to leave Delaware in 1850, only a

few states were open to them. Pennsylvania, New York, and
the New England states were viable options, for slavery had
been abolished there. Canada, where many fugitives on the
Underground Railroad had found homes, was also a possible
destination. Some nominally free states, among them Ohio,
Indiana, Illinois, and Oregon, were less inviting, for laws there
barred blacks from crossing their borders, although the laws
were not rigorously enforced.[46] Rhode Island was one of the
states where free blacks could relocate, and it was there that
the Tillman family headed.

Slavery had been practiced in Rhode Island and the other
New England states from early colonial days, but on a smaller
scale than in the Southern states.[47] Although wealthy shippers
and merchants in Boston, Providence, and Newport played
important roles in the transatlantic slave trade, transport-
ing many thousands of Africans from their native continent
to slavery in America, relatively few Africans were enslaved
locally.[48] The federal census of 1840 revealed only five slaves
in Rhode Island. The state had begun a program of gradual
abolition in 1784, and it was finally completed in 1842.[49]

Residents of Rhode Island exhibited an early aversion to
slavery, allowing the black slaves in their midst to achieve freedom rather easily. But as we have seen, granting slaves freedom was not the equivalent of giving them equal rights. Rhode
Islanders, like other New Englanders, regarded blacks with a
mixture of contempt and fear that made it all but impossible to
treat them as equals. Thus they were not only denied the right
to vote and to hold public office but also excluded from the

militia and forced instead to labor on public works projects. They were, however, accorded some rights that blacks farther south were denied. They had access to the courts, for example, and they were permitted to engage in business.[50] More important, the local economy provided them with job opportunities that were not available elsewhere.

Rhode Island was one of the busiest maritime centers in the American colonies and a place where free blacks could find employment aboard ships. Seafaring was one of the few occupations open to free blacks in the first half of the nineteenth century, not just in New England but also in New York, Pennsylvania, and Delaware. In the South, slave labor was used to gather agricultural products from plantations for voyages to the North. Coastal shipping was therefore a thriving business, profitable not only for the producers of the goods and the crops but also for the shippers.[51]

Tillman had probably never been to any kind of school, at least not long enough to acquire the rudiments of formal learning, for he could neither read nor write. Illiteracy was pervasive among blacks, free as well as slave, but also among many whites in Southern states. (Some slave masters even in Delaware were unable to read or to write their own names.)[52]

Even so, Tillman knew that there were opportunities for free black men on the ships that plied the coastal waters and regularly crossed the Atlantic to foreign destinations. The harbor at Providence was a busy center of maritime trade, and there was lots of shipping business on nearby Long Island. Ships built on Long Island were prominent in the robust maritime trade of the port of New York, only a little farther away.

William Tillman went to sea when he was fourteen years old and continued to work in the shipping industry for the next twelve or thirteen years.[53] When fully grown, he stood five feet eleven inches tall. He had short black hair, a high forehead, a strong, athletic build, and a dark complexion scarred with pockmarks. Though he spoke with the accent characteristic of most African Americans—a tone and manner of pronunciation sometimes dismissed as "black dialect"—his speech still had what a New York newspaper reporter later described as "a simple eloquence and force of its own."[54] He was employed by Jonas Smith & Co. when the Civil War broke out, and it was in that capacity that he sailed aboard the *S. J. Waring* in July 1861. The voyage promised to be a great adventure in the young black man's life. But as events would soon demonstrate, it would also be a dramatic chapter in the history of the war— and of the country.

TO SEA

We do not know precisely when William Tillman first began working on boats. In the court testimony he gave after his return to New York in 1861, he said that he had "been to sea all my days."[1] This could mean that he began to work on ships that sailed up and down the Delaware River when he was still in his early teens. It almost certainly indicates that he was employed on ships after he and his family moved to Rhode Island around 1850. And his own statement that he had been employed by Jonas Smith & Co. for four years before the *Waring* was captured indicates that he began to work for that firm when he was in his early twenties. Smith owned a large fleet of merchant vessels and was in a position to employ many men, black as well as white, on their voyages in and out of the port of New York.

Although the history of black mariners in early America is long and fascinating, it is little known. Small boats and sailing vessels had for many centuries provided men in their native Africa with opportunities to travel by water, navigating through streams and rivers and along that continent's thousands of miles of Atlantic coastline. Transported to colonial

America, African slaves took readily to the creeks, swamps, rivers, and inland waterways that laced the coastline of North America. They were put to work on canoes, skiffs, rafts, and barges, and even on sailing vessels—and not surprisingly, for slaves did virtually all the work in the early colonial days. Plantation owners depended on them not only to plant, tend, and harvest the agricultural products of the region but also to transport those products to the large sailing vessels that crowded Southern ports waiting to take them north, or even across the ocean, where healthy profits awaited. As cotton production became more profitable in the early nineteenth century, American shipping rapidly expanded, employing more than one hundred thousand men per year, about one-fifth of whom were blacks—some slaves but many free.[2]

In Massachusetts, Rhode Island, and New York, free blacks most often worked as cooks and stewards, positions that whites were loath to occupy because, given the prevailing attitudes of the time, they were not deemed "manly."[3] The shipboard duties of cooks and stewards were regulated by customs as well as the stern, sometimes cruel, discipline of shipmasters.[4] Firm discipline was, of course, essential on all seagoing vessels, for the safety of the vessel, the cargo, and the crew often depended on instant obedience to commands.[5] The black cooks and stewards were largely confined to specified quarters of the vessels they worked on—pantries, larders, and galleys—although when "all hands" were summoned they had to join other crew members in pulling and hauling ropes, sails, and anchor lines.[6]

Free blacks did not object to the positions they were assigned, because better job opportunities were rarely if ever available. Further, they enjoyed some prerogatives that other crew members did not. Because they were almost always employed as cooks and stewards, they did not have to compete with whites for those positions. The jobs were theirs as a kind of entitlement, and their domains were not to be intruded upon by anyone but the shipmaster.[7]

Jonas Smith & Co. had roots on the north shore of Long Island, though much of their shipping business was done in New York City. They occupied offices a block from the East River waterfront near the southern tip of Manhattan Island. Jonas Smith himself was a prominent citizen in Stony Brook, a small village in the town of Brookhaven, Suffolk County, Long Island, about sixty miles east of New York City, although he had business interests—and owned ships—in much of the surrounding area. Born in a neighboring village in 1794, Smith had come to Stony Brook as a young man with practically no money and little education.[8] This part of the north shore of Long Island was deeply indented with harbors that provided good launching sites for ships. The harbors faced Long Island Sound, a major waterway that was largely protected from the bitter winds and surf that pounded the south shore of Long Island. Because treacherous sandbars laced the waters of Stony Brook Harbor, it provided shelter only for small boats and shallow-draft schooners, while its neighbor, Port Jefferson, located about five miles to the east, was a deepwater port that accommodated much larger vessels.[9] Between Stony Brook and Port Jefferson was another village called Setauket. As Port Jefferson and Setauket became thriving shipbuilding centers, Stony Brook housed workers, warehouses, and shops as well as some shipbuilding yards. A few of the ships that Jonas Smith owned were built in Stony Brook proper, but many more in Setauket and Port Jefferson.[10]

Jonas Smith's early days in Stony Brook are imperfectly recorded. He may personally have commanded some ships while he was still a young man, for he was sometimes referred to as "Captain" Jonas Smith. He may also have engaged in some shipbuilding, though he is not listed in histories of the area as one of the principal builders. It was as a shipowner that he was best known, and for the wealth that he accumulated. At least by the 1850s, he owned a good part of the real estate in Stony Brook, had charge of docks facing Stony Brook Harbor, and was the owner of a fleet of oceangoing vessels that regularly left the port of New York for trading voyages along the Atlantic Coast.[11] He kept a home in Stony Brook, but spent most of his time in another house in Brooklyn, closer to his ships and adjacent to a chandlery (maritime supply store) that he operated for the benefit of sailors and shipowners.[12] An article published in the *Brooklyn Daily Eagle* some years after his death stated that he was "the largest Long Island vessel owner in the days when the business was in its prime. . . . His vessels sailed out on almost every sea." The article listed forty-four vessels owned by Smith, with their names and dates of construction. The *S. J. Waring*, the ship that William Tillman rescued from Confederate privateers in July 1861, was listed under the date 1853.[13]

The *S. J. Waring* was a schooner, built at Setauket by a prominent local shipbuilder named William Bacon.[14] Rigged fore and aft (without any square sails), it had two masts and a "full" rather than a "sharp" hull (one designed to maximize its carrying capacity rather than its speed). Its beam (width) was 29 feet, its length 119 feet, and its draft (depth in the water) 12 feet. Built of white oak, it was listed as a first-class vessel in the *American Lloyd's Registry*, a compendium of ship inspections and evaluations kept by maritime insurers. Its tonnage was given as 372, which, because it was a "full" model, enabled it to carry that weight plus an additional 75 percent, or something in the neighborhood of 650 tons.[15] It was named for Samuel J. Waring, a prominent maritime insurance executive and inspector who maintained offices on Wall Street, not far from Jonas Smith's shipping offices.[16]

Insurance was, of course, indispensable for mercantile shippers, who put great amounts of wealth at risk every time they sent a ship to sea. Without insurance, maritime shipping would be financially impossible. Samuel J. Waring (often called "Captain" Waring, like Jonas Smith) was one of the directors of the New York Fire and Marine Insurance Company.[17] He also checked ships to be sure they were in good condition before policies were issued, and was an official who was called on to give opinions about the placement of lighthouses in and around large coastal harbors.[18] Waring was probably a friend, as well as a valued business associate, of Jonas Smith, and for this reason won recognition as the namesake of one of Smith's vessels. The *Waring*'s captain was Francis "Frank" Smith, an experienced shipmaster who hailed from the village of Patchogue on the south shore of Long Island.

The *Waring*, like other schooners in the Jonas Smith fleet, was regularly employed in the coastal trade, sailing as far north as Maine and as far south as Florida, even going to Cuba when business carried it there. It made frequent calls in Charleston, South Carolina; Savannah, Georgia; and Fernandina, Florida.[19] Schooners were the favored vessels for the coastal trade because they could be manned by modest crews of officers and seamen, while full-rigged ships required larger and more expensive crews.

While employed by Jonas Smith, Tillman had made voyages to Southern ports, where he saw slaves working on the docks. In Delaware, in Rhode Island, and in New York he became acquainted with other blacks, some of whom were slaves or former slaves, or knew slaves and had tales to tell about their lives. Tillman thus learned much about the conditions that slaves endured.

Working conditions for free blacks who came down the coast from the North were rarely favorable. They were confined aboard ship for long periods, sometimes months, without ever setting foot on dry land. Their rations were severely restricted, as was their consumption of fresh water. All seamen had to endure the arbitrary discipline of ships' officers who were subject only to the most minimal oversight.[20] When they spoke to a vessel's officers, seamen were compelled to

address them by their surname with "Mr." prefixed and "Sir"
added.[21] The slightest disregard of an officer's order, even a
disrespectful comment, could result in solitary confinement,
denial of rations, or even flogging.[22] Black men suffered more
than whites from the disciplinary system, for racial prejudice
was never far from the ships, even those with home ports in
the North. When their vessels arrived in Southern ports, the
blacks also had to contend with local regulations. Free blacks
were often prevented from leaving the ships when they were in
port—forbidden to mingle with the slaves who worked on the
docks for fear they would plant the seeds of discontent in them.

In 1822 in South Carolina, the white fear and contempt
for African Americans found legal expression in an "Act for
the Better Regulation and Government of Free Negroes and
Persons of Color." Passed that year by the state legislature,
the law stated that "if any vessel shall come into any port or
harbour of this State, from any other State or foreign port,
having on board any free negroes or persons of color as cooks,
stewards, mariners, or in any other employment on board of
said vessel, such free negroes or persons of color shall be liable
to be seized and confined in jail until said vessel shall clear out
and depart from this State." When the vessel was ready to sail,
the captain was "bound to carry away the said free negro or
person of color, and to pay the expenses of his detention." If
he failed to do this, he was subject to a thousand-dollar fine
and two months in jail. The free blacks were subject to much
more severe penalties, for the law provided that they would be
"deemed and taken as absolute slaves, and sold."[23]

When U.S. Attorney General William Wirt (a Virginian) condemned the South Carolina law as unconstitutional, Governor John Wilson responded defiantly that his state had "the right to interdict the entrance of such persons into her ports . . . in the same manner as she can prohibit those afflicted with infectious diseases, to touch her shores."[24] The South Carolina law was later softened by substituting whipping for sale, and allowing blacks to remain belowdecks during the whole time their ships were in port. But the jails in which free blacks were confined were often on the docks or so near them that the free blacks in the holds of the visiting ships could hear the anguished cries that emanated from them. The South Carolina statute was soon imitated in other Southern states. North Carolina, Georgia, Florida, Louisiana, and eventually even the Spanish islands in the Caribbean passed their own versions of what came to be known as Negro Seamen's Acts, hoping to silence the same kind of communication that South Carolina had attempted to prevent.[25]

As an African American who was unable to read or write, William Tillman could not have known all the terrible details of the treatment accorded his African brothers in the American South. He could hear, however, and remember what he heard.

At 4:30 a.m. on the morning of Friday, April 12, 1861, the harbor of Charleston, South Carolina, erupted in a storm of cannon and artillery fire. In the six short weeks that followed the March 4 inauguration of Abraham Lincoln as president of the United States, seven states in the Deep South had adopted ordinances severing the legal ties that bound them to the Union, and the government of the newly created Confederate States of America had been organized in Montgomery, Alabama. Jefferson Davis of Mississippi, elected president of the Confederacy, had sent Gen. P. G. T. Beauregard of Louisiana to Charleston to compel the surrender of United States forts there.

Perched on a shoal at the mouth of Charleston Harbor, Fort Sumter was the target of the bombardment unleashed on that fateful morning by Beauregard and the thousands of militiamen he commanded. For thirty-three hours an estimated four thousand shots and shells showered down on Sumter. The small Union garrison inside the fort's walls responded with a thousand rounds from the forty-eight mounted guns at their disposal, but their commander, Maj. Robert Anderson of Kentucky, anticipated the outcome. On Sunday, April 14, Anderson formally lowered the Stars and Stripes in surrender.[26]

Abraham Lincoln responded promptly. On Monday, April 15, he issued a proclamation declaring that combinations "too powerful to be suppressed by the ordinary course of judicial proceedings, or by the powers vested in the Marshals by law," had arisen in South Carolina, Georgia, Alabama, Florida, Mississippi, Louisiana, and Texas, and calling for 75,000 state militiamen "to suppress said combinations and to cause the laws to be duly executed." He said that the purpose of the militia call was "to maintain the honor, the integrity, and the existence of the National Union, and the perpetuity of popular government," but he added (unwisely, as he later conceded) that "the first service to the forces hereby called forth will probably be to re-possess the forts, places, and property which have been seized from the Union." Privately Lincoln admitted that the troops he called for would first be needed to defend Washington against likely Confederate attack.[27]

Lincoln's proclamation met with prompt and positive responses. In Massachusetts, Ohio, Indiana, and other Northern states, the governors ordered state militia regiments to head south to defend the Union.[28] In New York City an estimated quarter of a million people gathered to express their support for the president and his action.[29] But unfavorable responses also came quickly. Virginia lost no time in adopting an ordinance of secession, thus joining its sister states farther south in defiance of Lincoln's call for unity. Riots greeted Massachusetts militiamen when they attempted to pass through Baltimore on April 19, and sixteen men (four militiamen and twelve Baltimoreans) were killed in the resulting melee.[30] Jefferson Davis also responded quickly to Lincoln's proclamation with one of his own.

On April 17, the same day that Virginia seceded from the Union, the Confederate president invited applications for "commissions or letters of marque and reprisal" authorizing privately owned vessels to be armed and sent to sea to attack Northern ships. Davis said that Lincoln had announced his intention of "invading this Confederacy with an armed force for the purpose of capturing its fortresses, and thereby subverting its independence and subjecting the free people thereof to the dominion of a foreign power." Letters of marque and reprisal would authorize private shipowners to help the Confederate states resist "so wanton and wicked an aggression." In his proclamation Davis called on all Confederate officials to be "vigilant and zealous" in their support of measures "for the common defense, and by which under the blessings of Divine Providence, we may hope for a speedy, just, and honorable peace."[31]

By April 19 events were proceeding at a rapid pace. The same day as the Baltimore riot, Lincoln responded to Davis's call for letters of marque and reprisal by issuing another proclamation, this one declaring a naval blockade of the Confederate coast. He noted that the leaders of the Southern "insurrection" had threatened to grant "pretended letters of marque" authorizing the bearers to commit "assaults on the lives, vessels, and property of good citizens of the country lawfully engaged in commerce on the high seas, and in waters of the United States." To resist these assaults, Lincoln said that a "competent force" would be posted to prevent the entrance and exit of vessels from the ports in secessionist states, and any person who committed such an assault would be "held amenable to the laws of the United States for the prevention and punishment of piracy."[32] Lincoln's invocation of the law of piracy was intended to send a stern message to anyone acting under one of the Confederacy's "pretended" letters of marque, for piracy had long been a capital offense under federal law: Anyone convicted of it faced a hangman's noose.[33]

The conflicting proclamations of Lincoln and Davis bore evidence of the sharp legal issues that divided the two men from the beginning of the war. Lincoln's call for militiamen revealed his conviction that the Southern secession was an "insurrection," not a valid assertion of national independence, and that its leaders had no right or authority to act as the leaders of a sovereign power. They had no right to attack or occupy federal forts or other properties. In contrast Jefferson Davis believed that Lincoln's effort to hold Southern forts was the aggression of a "foreign power" and that he, as leader of the independent Confederate government, had the authority to occupy federal properties within the Confederacy, and to attack them if their occupation was resisted. Davis also believed that he had the right and power to issue letters of marque and reprisal.[34]

Neither Lincoln nor Davis believed that privateering was in itself an illegal activity. The same clause of the U.S. Constitution that authorized Congress to declare war authorized it to "grant letters of marque and reprisal, and make rules concerning captures on land and water."[35] The Confederate constitution, which copied many provisions of the U.S. Constitution verbatim, contained an identical provision.[36] But letters of marque and reprisal granted by the Congress of the United States were not the same as those granted by an insurrectionist assembly only pretending to hold legislative powers. Lincoln believed that everything associated with the secessionist states and their government was tainted with illegality, and that Jefferson Davis was not promulgating real law but exercising a counterfeit authority grounded in insurrection.

Both Lincoln and Davis knew that privateering had played a role in previous American wars. In the long struggle against

Great Britain to establish American independence, privateers commissioned by the Continental Congress had provided some check on British shipping, then the greatest in the world. Privateers commissioned by the U.S. Congress had played a similar role in the War of 1812.[37] After that conflict was resolved, however, privateering fell into disuse and some disrepute. Privateers bore an unattractive resemblance to freebooters who roamed the seas looking for unarmed victims whose ships and cargoes could be taken for private profit. They were not government officers or employees. They received no government salaries and were subject only to the most minimal government control. They were entrepreneurs who outfitted and armed their own ships, gathered their own crews, and hoped to find enough booty afloat to make their enterprises profitable—while at the same time aiding the war efforts of the officials who commissioned them.

In 1856, at the conclusion of the Crimean War, the major naval powers of the world signed the Declaration of Paris, which laid down new international rules for maritime warfare. Agreed to by the United Kingdom, Austria, France, Prussia, Russia, Sardinia, and the Ottoman Empire, the declaration recognized that the uncertainties surrounding maritime law in time of war had "long been the subject of deplorable disputes." It accordingly declared that "privateering is and remains abolished." But the United States was not a signatory to the declaration and thus was not bound by it.[38]

Lincoln had no intention of commissioning privateers to roam the seas in the cause of preserving the Union. Jefferson

Davis, in contrast, believed that privateers would aid his cause because the North was the center of shipbuilding and shipping and gave every sign of remaining so, while the Confederacy had no navy and practically no means of acquiring one. To be sure, the U.S. Navy was not very large in early 1861, consisting of ninety ships, only forty-two of which were in commission, and they were widely scattered across the globe. Some were stationed in Atlantic ports, some off the coast of Brazil, some in the Mediterranean, and others as far away as the China Sea. There were only a dozen warships in American waters, and five were sailing vessels that would have a difficult time pursuing the new class of steam vessels that was beginning to appear in the Atlantic.[39] If the U.S. Navy was weak, however, the government over which Lincoln presided had the ability—and the determination—to make it grow.

The naval resources available to the Confederacy were much more meager. When war broke out a good number of U.S. naval officers loyal to the South resigned their commissions, giving Davis a substantial pool of experienced commanders to lead a sea force. But ships for them to command were almost nonexistent. Not only were there few merchant vessels in the South, but no naval vessels or enlisted men that could be put into immediate service. The Confederacy, however, did have one resource that it hoped to put to good use. The Gosport Navy Yard near Norfolk, Virginia, beleaguered by secessionist Virginia militiamen, had been abandoned by U.S. commanders on April 20. The militiamen promptly took over the yard, which included a functioning dry dock, more than a thousand cannons, and an impressive supply of shot and shells. The guns and ammunition were quickly seized and sent all over the South, where they could be used to fortify key locations on the coast and on navigable rivers. More important, Gosport also included the hulk of a steam frigate named the USS *Merrimack*. Although federal forces had scuttled the vessel before they left, enough of it remained to be rebuilt and reconstituted as the CSS *Virginia*. Yankees would insist on still calling it the *Merrimack* when, less than a year later, newly clad in iron armor and under Confederate command, it became one of the most famous vessels in the history of the Civil War by inflicting serious damage on Union vessels in Hampton Roads, Virginia, and fighting the ironclad USS *Monitor* in an epic naval duel.[40]

Lincoln's blockade and Jefferson Davis's solicitation of letters of marque and reprisal raised difficult problems for both men. Under accepted principles of international law, a blockade was valid only if it was declared by one nation against another with whom it was at war.[41] But Lincoln did not recognize the Confederacy as a nation separate and apart from the United States, and Congress never declared war against the Confederacy. The Confederacy in Lincoln's eyes was not a nation at war with the United States but merely a combination of insurrectionists. Further, it had been understood since the eighteenth century that foreign nations were legally bound to observe a blockade only if it was enforced by an adequate naval force. As expressed in the Declaration of Paris in 1856, a blockade required a force "sufficient really to prevent access to the coast of the enemy."[42] A blockade declared without adequate enforcement was nothing more than a "paper blockade" and not legally enforceable.[43]

Lincoln's difficulty was compounded by the fact that the Confederate coastline was much longer than the North's. After Virginia and North Carolina joined the other Confederate states in secession, Lincoln extended the blockade to include them.[44] This stretched the Confederate coast to 3,549 miles, the approximate distance from New York to Liverpool, and brought an astounding 189 harbors and coves within its purview.[45] Lincoln's secretary of the navy, Gideon Welles, was working furiously to expand the navy by buying ships, leasing some, and commissioning the construction of others. Under his prodding the nation's sea force was growing. But when Lincoln first declared his blockade, it was not adequate to post ships outside every Southern port and interdict all vessels attempting to enter and exit. Yet the very length of the Southern coastline exposed the Confederacy to Union attacks. Davis believed that privateers and the length of his coastline would give him an advantage in the war on the waters. Lincoln disagreed. In time, events would prove Davis wrong and Lincoln right—but only in time.

In his proclamation of April 17, Davis had outlined the procedures that applicants for letters of marque and reprisal would have to follow. They would be required to make a written statement "giving the name and a suitable description of the character, tonnage, and force of the vessel" they sought to convert to a privateer. Their application would have to name the place and residence of each of the owners of the vessel and the intended number of the crew. They would have to sign the statement and deliver it to the Confederate secretary of state, or to the collector of a Confederate port of entry, to be transmitted by him to the secretary of state. They would have to give a bond to the Confederacy in the sum of five thousand dollars, or if the vessel was to have more than 150 men aboard, ten thousand dollars, conditioned on their observance of "the laws of these Confederate states and the instructions given to them for the regulation of their conduct."[46]

There was a problem, however, for there were then no Confederate laws governing privateers. So Davis called a special session of the Confederate Congress, which met in the capitol at Montgomery, Alabama, on April 29. There he asked them for a declaration of war between the Confederate states and the "Government of the United States," and for a law authorizing privateers. He admitted that he had called for applications for letters of marque and reprisal before any laws on the subject were passed by Congress, and that Congress alone had the power under the Confederate constitution to authorize privateers. But that was a mere question of timing. "I entertain no doubt," he told the legislators, "that you will concur with me in the opinion that in the absence of a fleet of public vessels it will be eminently expedient to supply their place by private-armed vessels, so happily styled by the publicists of the United States 'the militia of the sea,' and so often and justly relied on by them as an efficient and admirable instruction of offensive warfare."[47] Congress did not act immediately—there were committee hearings to be held and amendments to be proposed and voted on—but a finished bill was put on President Davis's desk on May 6, at which time he signed it.[48]

The Confederate law on privateering was closely modeled on the United States statute.[49] It provided that ships and cargoes captured by privateers (called prizes) had to be brought into admiralty courts, where they would be condemned and sold at auction. One-twentieth of the proceeds would be paid into the public treasury, where it would be held in trust as a pension fund for disabled seamen. The rest of the money would be divided among the officers and crew. If they had provided by contract how the money would be divided, it would be distributed among them according to the contractual provisions. If they had not, one-half would go to the owners of the capturing vessel and one-half to the officers and crew.[50]

Beginning the day after Jefferson Davis's April 29 proclamation, applications for letters of marque and reprisal began to come into the secretary of state's office in Montgomery. Support for the secessionist cause was high in newspapers all over the Confederacy, and the support was reflected in many men who were eager to aid the cause by taking privately owned vessels to sea. Capturing Yankee ships could be very profitable as well as patriotic. Optimistic predictions of the success of Confederate privateers appeared in the newspapers. The *New Orleans Daily Crescent* declared that "at the lowest estimate, seven hundred and fifty swift-sailing, staunch, substantial vessels, fully equipped, carrying on an average four mighty guns apiece, can be put afloat in four months to wage war upon the Northern commerce, blockade Northern ports, cripple Northern strength and destroy Northern property."[51]

The first commission was given on May 10 to a small schooner from Brunswick, Georgia, called the *Triton*. It was rated at only thirty tons, but it mounted a six-pound swivel gun and carried a crew of thirty men. A much larger ship was fitted out at Wilmington, Delaware, two weeks later. A steamer of 1,644 tons named the *Phenix* (sic), it carried seven guns and had a complement of twenty-four officers and 219 crewmen.[52] Privateering ships typically carried much larger crews than ordinary merchant ships, for when a privateer captured an enemy vessel it had to put its own officers and men aboard. They formed what was called the prize crew, and it was their duty to take the captured vessel back to port to be condemned in an admiralty court. The more ships that were captured, the more men would be needed to fill out the prize crews.

On May 18 letters of marque were issued to a fifty-four-ton pilot boat in the Charleston Harbor that had been armed with one eighteen-pound gun and renamed the *Savannah*. Schooner rigged and displacing only 54 tons, the *Savannah* became the first privateer to leave the South Carolina port when it headed out to sea on June 3 with twenty men aboard. Good fortune crowned the *Savannah*'s efforts when, only two days out of Charleston, it came on a merchant brig from Rockland, Maine, called the *Joseph*, carrying a valuable cargo of sugar. The *Savannah* installed a prize crew on the captured vessel and sent it to Charleston, where the district court for the Confederate states would condemn it and its cargo as a prize. However, continuing on its search for enemy vessels, the *Savannah*'s luck quickly vanished. On the same day that it captured the *Joseph*, it crossed the path of the USS *Perry*, a well-armed Union man-of-war on blockade duty off the coast. After a brief exchange of fire, the *Savannah* was forced to surrender to the *Perry*, which claimed it as a prize of war and sent it to New York for proceedings in the U.S. District Court there.[53]

Letters of marque and reprisal were issued on June 18 to another vessel in Charleston Harbor. A brig of 187 tons measuring ninety-two feet and two inches in length and twenty-two feet and eight inches in breadth, it had been built in Baltimore in 1845 and made its first voyage to Philadelphia as the *Putnam*. Sold to new owners in Providence, Rhode Island, in 1850, it was reregistered in Boston in 1851, in New York in 1852, and in New Orleans in 1857. It was in the Louisiana city that it was renamed the *Echo*, painted black, and rigged in the French style with hempen sails. It was also in New Orleans that it began its short life as an illegal African slave trader, which ended abruptly when it was captured by a U.S. sloop of war off the coast of Cuba in December 1858 with more than three hundred slaves aboard. Condemned and resold to owners in Charleston, it resumed its name of *Putnam* and once again entered the merchant trade. With the outbreak of the war between the Confederacy and the United States, twenty local owners (or shareholders) in Charleston outfitted the vessel with five British cannons and assembled seventy officers and crewmen to man it; then they applied to the collector of customs in Charleston for letters of marque and reprisal. Originally slated to be named the *Rattlesnake*, the new privateer was rechristened the *Jefferson Davis*.[54] The name was understandable, for the vessel's owners held the president of the Confederate states in high esteem.

In the evening of June 28 the *Jefferson Davis*—often called the *Jeff Davis* by its affectionate admirers—sailed out of Charleston Harbor.[55] It left behind cheering crowds in the city but looked warily to sea for any sign of Union warships patrolling the harbor entrance. None could be seen, notwithstanding what the *Charleston Mercury* called "the very efficient blockade of Abraham I [using the roman numeral to indicate that Lincoln was a monarch or tyrant]."[56]

June 28 was an auspicious date in the history of the Confederacy, for the *Jefferson Davis* was destined to become its most celebrated privateer. It was also a notable date in the history of the United States, for it was the anniversary of a furious battle that took place in Charleston Harbor in 1776, when Revolutionary patriots fended off a British naval attack led by Adm. Sir Peter Parker. In the fighting that day, Parker's flagship was sunk, two hundred casualties and forty-six deaths were inflicted on his attacking force, and the admiral's own breeches were embarrassingly blown off by gunfire. June 28, 1861, was also an important date in the life of William Tillman, for he would soon encounter the *Jeff Davis* at sea and, as a consequence, earn a place for himself in the history of the Civil War.

THREE

THE CAPTURE

The men who sailed aboard the *Jefferson Davis* were an intriguing group. As captain of the privateer, Louis Mitchell Coxetter was the commander of the vessel, responsible for all of its maritime efforts. Coxetter's enthusiasm for the Confederate cause was never doubted, even though he was a Nova Scotian by birth and had what some described as a "slightly perceptible foreign accent." A story in the *New Orleans Daily Crescent* reported that he was "apparently a Holland Dutchman," although this may have been a misperception drawn from his accent.[1]

A stout man, Coxetter stood about five feet seven inches tall, was a little over forty years old, and wore a mustache and a goatee. Despite his slightly odd manner of speaking, the *Crescent* declared that he spoke English "very fluently" and that he issued his orders "in a very mild and calm tone." He wore no uniform and did not carry a sword, but "was attired in plain citizen's dress."[2] Coxetter's maritime experience had been gained as captain of small boats that traded in coastal waters, following the shoreline north and south of his home base in Charleston.

William Ross Postell was a more experienced seaman than Coxetter and, according to most observations, a more energetic man aboard ship. Born in 1818 in the Beaufort District of South Carolina, he had entered the U.S. Navy while still a young man. After serving on navy vessels for eight years, he resigned to take another position in the infant Texas navy. (The self-designated Republic of Texas claimed independent status from 1836 until its annexation by the United States in 1844.) His Texas superior reported that he was "one of the most valuable and efficient officers in the Navy," but he was not always easy to get along with. At one point Texas authorities announced their intention of bringing disciplinary charges against him, but they lacked proof, and when he demanded a raise in pay, they denied it. So he resigned and moved with his family to Savannah, where he worked for a time on merchant ships before taking a position in the Lighthouse and Buoy Service of the U.S. Treasury Department. Disciplinary problems again arose—Postell was apparently a hard drinker and not always willing to follow orders. In 1858 he took a position as a supercargo on a privately owned bark called the *E. A. Rawlins* that was suspected of involvement in the African slave trade. (The supercargo of a vessel takes no part in its navigation but handles its business transactions, buying what needs to be bought and collecting the proceeds of items that are sold.) Slave trading was condemned by the laws of the United States as well as Great Britain and France, but the laws were imperfectly enforced, with many a wink of the eye from Southern law enforcement authorities. They argued that the trade was not nearly as offensive as "Black Republicans" in the North claimed, and since slavery itself was fully defensible, there was nothing wrong with bringing more slaves to America. The *Rawlins* made at least one successful voyage carrying slaves from Africa to Cuba, possibly more. Postell's pay was eighty dollars per month, which was sent to his wife and family in Savannah. He also received two out of every hundred slaves that the *Rawlins* successfully landed.[3] After he acquired the slaves, he could put them up for sale in the very active slave auctions that thrived in Savannah and other towns and cities throughout the South.

The *New Orleans Daily Crescent* reported that Postell had a "moustache and slight whiskers" but wore no uniform and carried no sword. The *Crescent* described him as bearing "all the characteristics of an adventurer, with a dash of the hero. . . . Notwithstanding his years" (Postell was then in his early forties), he was "very lithe and active" and on board the *Davis* he was "a busier and more important personage than the captain."[4]

As to why Coxetter was named the captain of the *Jefferson Davis* and Postell designated as his first lieutenant, when Postell's naval experience and shipboard skills seemed the greater of the two, Postell's spotty job record probably did not help him, and the disciplinary incidents in his background were not assets. Another reason for his junior status may be more obvious: Coxetter was one of the owners of the *Jefferson Davis*.[5] He had enough money, or perhaps enough influence in Charleston, to be registered in the *Davis*'s papers as one of the twenty-seven owners of the privateer. In the letters of marque, which designated the shares each of the officers and crew members was entitled to (there were 126.75 shares in all), Coxetter was entitled to thirteen and Postell only to ten.[6] Postell never seemed to have much money and could not contribute to the store of cash and credit necessary to outfit the vessel for its entry into the very risky service of a privateer.[7]

The men who made up the balance of the *Davis*'s crew were a motley assemblage.[8] One observer thought that they were "as wretched a set of scoundrels as could be picked up in any seaport." They were all armed, but "they wore clothes of all shapes and sizes, and many of them were shoeless."[9] Capt. Frank Smith remembered that they were "a mixture of all nations, principally Irish and Dutch."[10] Some had acquired places on the privateer because they supported the secessionist cause and wanted to help disrupt Lincoln's blockade of the Southern coast. Some were adventurers who hoped to gain a share of the profits that the privateer could make. Others were down on their luck and desperate for any opportunity to make some money.

The *Jeff Davis*'s first two days out of Charleston were uneventful. It encountered no other ships—most important, none of the Union vessels then attempting to enforce the coastal blockade. This was not surprising, for the U.S. Navy was spread very thin, and it was impossible for it to effectively patrol all the Southern ports subject to its watch. On Sunday, June 30, however, a lookout high on the *Jeff Davis*'s masthead sighted a vessel in the distance. It was an intriguing craft and seemed worth pursuing, but problems with the privateer's overhead gearing interfered with efforts to do so, and the vessel soon disappeared. Later in the same day, another vessel was sighted, but closer examination revealed it to be French, so it was allowed to proceed without interference. The *Jeff Davis* was looking for Yankee vessels, not those of any European power.

For another week the privateer sailed north along the coast of the Carolinas, propelled by the winds and the warm waters of the Gulf Stream, the powerful sea current that originates in the Gulf of Mexico, rounds the tip of Florida, and flows north along the coast of North America as far as Newfoundland before crossing the ocean toward Europe. On Thursday, July 4, Captain Coxetter ordered the Confederate flag run up the mainmast. It was the eighty-fifth anniversary of American independence—the first since the secession of the Southern states—and the day that was celebrated throughout the country as the birthday of American freedom. A salute was fired, and glasses were raised to celebrate the occasion. Then a sail suddenly appeared off the bow. Drawing near the vessel, the Confederates fired a warning shot. The vessel halted, permitting the privateers to determine that it was an English brig so—like the French vessel—it too was dismissed.[11]

In the evening of the Fourth, another ship was spied, but it proved to be a brig from Baltimore, so it was also permitted to continue on its way without interference. The Confederacy was not at war with Maryland, was it? Although Maryland was still a part of the Union, it was, like South Carolina, a slaveholding state, and the privateers entertained hopes that it would soon secede and join its Southern brethren in the Confederacy.[12]

On the morning of Saturday, July 6, the *Jeff Davis* captured its first prize. It was about three hundred miles east of southern Delaware when it spied sails in the distance and judged them to belong to a Yankee brig. Drawing near, it fired a shot that forced the brig to halt. The privateers came aboard and learned that the vessel was a Yankee merchantman from Philadelphia bearing the name *John Welsh*. It was en route from the Caribbean island of Trinidad to Falmouth, England, carrying a rich cargo of sugar. When the *Welsh*'s captain informed Postell that the sugar was Spanish property, Postell scoffed: "You are our prize, and the Spaniards have no business to ship their cargoes in American bottoms." After a large part of the *Welsh*'s provisions and stores were transferred to the privateer, a prize crew was installed and the vessel was sent to Savannah, where the district court would condemn it as a prize and the marshal would sell it at auction.[13] The officers and crew of the *Welsh* were taken aboard the *Jeff Davis* as prisoners.[14]

July 6 proved to be a profitable day for the *Davis*, for not long after the *Welsh* was captured another Yankee vessel was spied, pursued, and brought to a halt. This was the *Enchantress*, a schooner out of Newburyport, Massachusetts, on its way from Boston to Santiago de Cuba loaded with provisions, grindstones, glassware, and lumber.[15] Another prize crew was installed on the *Enchantress* with orders to take it to Savannah, where the proceeds would be distributed among the officers and crew of the privateer.[16] As in the case of the *Welsh*, the officers and all the men of the *Enchantress* were taken aboard the *Jeff Davis*—all the men, that is, except the black cook and steward, one Jacob Garrick. The decision to leave Garrick on the *Enchantress* would later prove to be a critical mistake.[17]

While the *Jeff Davis* was sailing up the coast in search of Yankee vessels it could capture, preparations were under way in New York for the imminent departure of the *S. J. Waring* on a long commercial voyage to Uruguay and Argentina. Customs officials had cleared the schooner from the port on July 3 and, in the early morning hours of July 4, it pulled away from its dock on the East River and, with a harbor pilot at the wheel, headed out to sea.[18]

July 4, 1861, proved to be nearly as auspicious a day in New York as June 28, 1861, had been in Charleston, for the people of the city were determined to celebrate the national holiday. To be sure, New York was not a fervent center of Unionist sentiment in 1861. The city's commercial dependence on cotton shipments from the South had strongly influenced its political life, which was dominated by the Democratic Party. In October 1860 the Democrats had gathered in a mass meeting in the Cooper Union, proclaimed themselves the "white man's party," and angrily charged that the Republicans were planning to abolish slavery in the nation.[19] In the election of November 1860 presidential candidate Abraham Lincoln was outpolled in every ward in the city, although he received enough upstate support to give him the state's electoral votes. "What would New York be without slavery?" an English journal asked provocatively, to which James De Bow, a Louisianian and one of the strongest and most vocal proslavery advocates in the nation, answered emphatically: "The ships would rot at the docks; the grass would grow in Wall Street and Broadway, and the glory of New York, like that of Babylon and Rome, would be numbered with the things of the past."[20]

New York's mayor, Fernando Wood, seemed to agree with De Bow when, in January 1861, he proposed that New York City secede from both New York State and the United States. Under Wood's plan New York would become a "free city" and thus be able to continue its trade with the South despite the war then brewing between the sections.[21] His proposal did not gain enough support to prevail, but it reflected a lot of political opinion in the nation's largest city. New York's population in the 1860 census was 814,254. That number included 12,574 blacks, most of whom were unable to vote because of property requirements.[22] Housing was segregated along racial lines, and jobs for African Americans were next to nonexistent. When a statewide proposal for universal suffrage was placed on the ballot, it was rejected by 95 percent of the voters in the city, and James Gordon Bennett, the influential editor and publisher of the *New York Herald*, issued a call for the reenslavement of Northern blacks.[23] Sympathy for the Republican Party's plan to end slavery in America—gradually but certainly—was minimal. After the Confederate attack on Fort Sumter, however, sentiment seemed to change. The question then was not whether slavery should be abolished but whether the United States should be broken apart. "We are either for the country or for its enemies," the president of the New York Chamber of Commerce declared.[24]

As the *Waring* left its dock on that July 4, patriotic feeling surged in New York. Bands played, and troops marched in the streets (though most of the local militia had already left to answer Lincoln's call for volunteers). The statesman and orator Edward Everett, who was to share the rostrum with Lincoln at Gettysburg a little over two years later, came down from Boston to deliver a speech at the Academy of Music on East Fourteenth Street on "The Great Issues Now Before the Country." Patriotic flags flew from hotels and public buildings, and fireworks were discharged into the night sky. Reporting on the celebration, the *New York Times* called it "a great National thanksgiving...a pious opportunity for recognizing a great political fact, rendered peculiarly impressive by the circumstance that for the moment it has been blindly, madly forgotten by our brothers in a portion of the still smiling land."[25]

In addition to the pilot, nine men were aboard the *Waring* as it left on its long southern voyage. The captain was Frank Smith, the first mate Timothy J. Smith, and the second mate Charles Davidson.[26] The crew consisted of four seamen. William Tillman was the cook and steward. An Irish passenger named Bryce MacKinnon was also aboard, with passage for Montevideo. The pilot navigated the schooner through the harbor and the Narrows and, when the ocean was safely reached, debarked for his pilot boat.[27] The schooner's cargo hold was fully laden.[28]

It took three days for the *Waring* to pass through the Gulf Stream.[29] Powered only by the wind in their sails, vessels bound on long voyages to the south could not battle the current along the coast, so they routinely headed out to sea to avoid its flow before turning southward.

By Sunday, July 7, 1861, the *Waring* had progressed about two hundred miles to the south and east of Sandy Hook, the barrier peninsula that guards the entrance to New York Harbor.[30] The weather on the trip out was "tolerably fair."[31] About midway through the morning, the officers and crew sighted sails on the horizon. They continued sailing until ten o'clock, when the first mate told Captain Smith he thought they should alter their course, as he "did not like the look" of the sighted vessel. Smith declined to do so, but he took out his telescope and peered into the distance. He could see that an odd-looking brig was approaching. Its hull was painted black but stained with rust; its sails were of brownish hemp rather than the white cotton canvas common on English and American vessels.[32] And a French flag was flying from its mast. The brig was about a quarter of a mile away when, a little past noon, it fired a warning shot.

A swivel gun amidships—previously concealed beneath a thick canvas covering—was now clearly visible to Captain Smith.[33] And there were four other guns, two on each of the vessel's sides. The *Waring* was unarmed, so it quickly hove to, for failure to do so would provoke further shots, not designed to warn but to inflict real damage on the schooner.[34] The *Waring*'s officers thought at first that the approaching vessel might have been a French man-of-war "seeking news from the States."[35] Very quickly, however, they learned otherwise: It was the privateer *Jeff Davis*.

A boat was lowered from the *Davis*'s starboard side loaded with a crew of men who approached the *Waring* and quickly came aboard. The officer in charge was the first lieutenant, William Ross Postell. Facing Captain Smith, Postell announced: "We have taken you as a prize to the brig *Jeff Davis*, bearing letters of marque of the Confederate States." Then, pointing to the Stars and Stripes that flew over the *Waring*, he issued an order: "Haul down that flag!"[36]

Watching the encounter, William Tillman immediately realized that Smith and Postell knew each other.[37] Both had experience sailing in waters along the southern coast and had probably become acquainted there. As the American flag was taken down, the French flag on the *Jeff Davis* was also lowered—it had been a ruse, a common tactic employed by both pirates and privateers to deceive their intended targets—and the banner of the Confederate states was run up.[38]

Postell informed Captain Smith that he and his crew had been captured, that the *Waring* and its cargo were now prizes of war under the control of the Confederate States of America. They were to be taken south, he said, to Charleston, or some nearby point along the Confederate coast.[39]

The two officers then went into the schooner's cabin, where

they exchanged their papers. Examining the *Jeff Davis*'s letters of marque, Smith bowed to the inevitable and surrendered the *Waring* to the privateers. The Yankee captain was a gentleman, so he brought out brandy and glasses and shared drinks with Postell.[40] Then he watched as the privateering crew opened the schooner's hatches and rifled through its equipment and stores.

The crewmen immediately saw that the *Waring*'s cargo was valuable. They took some items for immediate transfer to the *Davis*, it being customary for both pirates and privateers to help themselves to food, water, tools, tackle, even furniture— anything that might help to sustain their marauding voyage without the necessity of touching land. Among other things, they carried off some of the *Waring*'s plates and coffee cups, a lot of tablecloths, a quantity of flour, several oilcans, a tub of butter, some cases of preserved lobster, and all the firearms they could find.[41] Tillman had concealed a hatchet in his cabin, though it is doubtful whether he initially considered it a weapon or merely a tool he could use in carrying out his shipboard duties, and the Confederates did not detect it.

The boat used to carry men and stores between the two ships was kept busy for an hour or so. In that time five men were taken off the *Waring*—the three officers and two crew members—and five were transferred from the privateer to the schooner.[42] The five men brought aboard were now designated as the prize officers and crew. Only three of the *Waring*'s original crew were left aboard. They were a German sailor named William Stedding, a Canada-based Scot named Donald McLeod, and Tillman, the cook and steward. The Irish passenger, Bryce MacKinnon, also remained in place.[43] The men taken aboard the *Jeff Davis* were Captain Smith, first mate Timothy J. Smith, and second mate Charles Davidson.[44] Captain Smith also had one of his sons on the *Waring*, and he was taken with his father onto the *Davis*.[45]

When Captain Smith and four of his men were taken to the *Davis* as prisoners, Montague Amiel was installed on the *Waring* as its prize captain. Little is known about Amiel except that he was a native of North Carolina who had moved to Charleston, where he worked as a harbor pilot. He was apparently in his thirties in 1861, although his exact age isn't clear. George Stephens, an Irishman, was the first mate, and a South Carolinian named Malcolm Liddy the second mate. James Milnor, another South Carolinian, and James Dorsett, who hailed from New Jersey, were the seamen who rounded out the prize crew.[46]

The capture completed and the prize crew installed, Postell and the remaining crew from the *Jeff Davis* returned to their brig, ready to resume their privateering voyage in search of more Yankee prizes.

With its captors in command, the *Waring* now headed south. Although Stedding, McLeod, and Tillman were designated as prisoners, they were not restrained, for they were expected to continue to perform their shipboard duties as they had before the capture. MacKinnon may also have been considered a prisoner, although his status was distinct from that of the seamen. He later said that he "became quite intimate with the officers," although he expected he would soon become a prisoner of war in Charleston.

Tillman, Stedding, and McLeod took care to behave themselves as they did their work, for they knew that any resistance to the prize crew could result in terrible consequences. Tillman cooked for everybody on the schooner. He served their meals, cleaned their cabins and staterooms, and performed whatever other duties he was given. He did not speak to the officers unless he was first spoken to, and he never questioned their orders. Life aboard the schooner—as aboard merchant vessels all around the Atlantic—was ritualized, and Tillman knew the ritual.[47] William Stedding and Donald McLeod were similarly careful of their work habits, while the passenger, Bryce MacKinnon, watched as they did their work and, in leisure hours, engaged in friendly conversations with the Confederate officers.[48]

As soon as the privateers began their southern voyage, they began to make a rebel flag out of the American banner that had been taken down from the schooner's mast. They cut up the flag, reassembled the pieces, and made them into what passed for a rebel insignia. (An ability to handle a needle and thread was one of the skills that seamen commonly cultivated, for in their long voyages at sea they often had to darn socks, mend worn or torn clothes, or repair tattered sails. Sewing was regarded as women's work on land, but at sea men did it without grumbling.) Tillman watched as the privateers took the Stars and Stripes apart and fashioned a Confederate banner from it, and he grew angry. He later recalled that the sight inspired him with an "incentive of revenge."[49]

As Tillman and his fellow captives performed their shipboard duties, they kept their eyes on the prize captain, his two mates, and his two sailors. They studied their habits, noted when they went to sleep at night and when they arose in the morning, memorized the pattern of their work. And they scanned the horizon for any sign of distant ships. They knew they might encounter other Confederate privateers, sent out to capture commercial vessels from the North like the *Waring*. If they encountered such ships, they would be doomed, for the crews aboard them and the guns they carried would reinforce the power of the *Jeff Davis*. But they hoped they might encounter a Yankee cruiser, perhaps one of the forty or so vessels the Union navy had in service at the outset of the war. They prayed that such a cruiser might overpower the captured *Waring*, rescue the captive crewmen aboard, and take the privateers in chains to a Northern port, where they would face stern Yankee justice. But no ships, either Confederate or Yankee, appeared. As the schooner proceeded steadily southward, their chances of being rescued were growing steadily smaller.

It seemed clear from the start why the Confederates had left Tillman on the *Waring* while they took other crew members off. As the ship's cook and steward, he would of course perform valuable services for the privateers. Beyond that, however, he was the only black on the vessel. When the *Waring* reached its Southern destination, the schooner and all the

property it carried would be sold at public auction. The Confederates believed that a slave was property and that, because
Tillman was black and a prisoner of war, he was a candidate
for slavery. They could sell him with other items of property
they took from the *Waring*. What's more, he would bring a
good price when he was sold, for he was young and strong, and
after the sale was done the privateers would, under terms of
the *Jefferson Davis*'s letters of marque, all share in the proceeds
of the sale.[50]

Evidence that the privateers intended to sell Tillman into
slavery emerged soon after the *Waring* fell under their control.
Before Postell left the schooner, he had a short conversation
with the steward. Tillman later recalled that Postell was "sitting in the cabin, cross-legged, smoking," when "he said to me,
when you go down to Savannah, I want you to go to my house,
and I will take care of you." If he went to Postell's "house" he
might be expected to work as a slave there, or merely be prepared for transport to the local slave auction. Neither option
appealed to him. Yes, you will take care of me, when you get
me there, Tillman thought. "I raised my hat and said: 'Yes,
Sir, thank you.' But afterward [I] said to Billy, the German,
I am not going to Charleston a live man; they may take me
there dead."[51]

Earlier, in the presence of both Captain Smith and the
steward, Postell made another disturbing comment about Tillman, saying: "We will take care of that fellow for about 1,000
or 1,200 dollars when we get him there." Tillman recognized

this as the going price for a healthy slave in Southern slave markets. His reaction to this statement was similarly guarded, but defiant.[52]

Tillman once heard Captain Amiel speak of the price he would bring when they reached the South. The captain told one of his crew to "talk to the steward and keep him in good heart," adding: "By God, he will never see the North again."[53]

MacKinnon offered support for Tillman's suspicions about the prize captain's intentions when he recalled that Amiel "had congratulated himself upon the valuable prize he had found in the steward, whom he vowed was worth a cool thousand on Meeting Street, Charleston." (Meeting Street was the principal commercial thoroughfare of the South Carolina city and the location of a busy slave market.) And MacKinnon remembered that "on several occasions" Tillman "shook his head and muttered, 'Dem fo'ks neber git to Charles'n.' "[54]

MacKinnon was not privy to all of the black steward's thoughts as the *Waring* sailed south, or to the plans he was laying to avoid the fate that awaited him when the *Waring* reached its Southern port. The Irishman's friendliness with the privateers had persuaded the steward that he could not safely confide in him.[55] But with each passing day, Tillman's hopes of a U.S. naval rescue grew dimmer, and his determination to rescue himself—or at least try to—grew stronger. He could not forget the threats that Postell and Amiel had made to him. And he was unable to forget the stories he heard, the acquaintances he encountered, the many voyages he made along the

Southern coast—all of which had instilled in him a grim understanding of what it meant to be a slave in the American South. He may not have remembered the words verbatim, but as he brooded over his plight and his chances of avoiding it, he surely nurtured the thoughts that had provoked him to tell MacKinnon: "Dem fo'ks neber git to Charles'n."[56]

FOUR

NOW IS OUR TIME

As the *Waring* sailed southward, Tillman began to work out a plan to avoid the fate that lay ahead of him. He knew that he would have to wait for an opportune moment to act—when the risk of being turned on and summarily killed would not be too great—and he had to have some help.

One afternoon, when the work of the ship occupied the attention of the Confederates, Tillman approached William Stedding in a place where the two men could speak confidentially. He had reason to believe that the German sailor was sympathetic to his plight, for his own future was clouded. When the *Waring* reached its Southern destination, Stedding feared that he might be regarded as a prisoner of war, put behind bars or impressed into military service for the Confederate army, and he dreaded that fate as much as Tillman dreaded being sold into slavery. "I am willing to do anything to clear myself out of slavery and to clear yourself, too," Tillman told Stedding. "I don't intend to go into slavery a live man. That is one thing certain. If fighting will clear us out of this trouble, I am willing to fight or do anything else to take the vessel."[1]

The German listened sympathetically. "I don't want to see you go into slavery," he told Tillman, "and I don't want to go there myself." He said he would ask McLeod if he would help them. Stedding approached the Scot and, taking care not to be overheard, inquired if he would join them in an effort to take back the schooner. McLeod said he would have "no hand in it," for when he got to a Southern port, he and the Irish MacKinnon—both of whom were subjects of Queen Victoria—would call for the intervention of the British consul, who would persuade the Confederates to release them.[2] That would be enough to protect their freedom.

Since neither Tillman nor Stedding could look forward to a British rescue, they realized they would have to act alone. It was, Stedding said, their "only chance." "Yes," Tillman replied, "this is our only chance." If they didn't take the schooner back from the Confederates, the steward said they would have to "go into a southern port to be pressed into slavery, or have our heads chopped off, I don't know which." [3]

Determined not to let that happen, Tillman approached McLeod and again asked if he would help him and Stedding. But the Scot repeated his refusal. Tillman then told Stedding that they would have to act by themselves, even if they lost their lives in the attempt. Stedding agreed, saying: "It is the same with me as it is with you."[4]

Tillman now outlined his plan to the German: When Stedding took the wheel, as he typically did at night, Tillman would retire to his stateroom berth in the schooner's cabin. He would do this at about ten o'clock, as was his habit, so the privateers would not suspect that anything unusual was about to happen. With Stedding at the wheel, the first mate would be nearby on watch. After the captain and second mate had both retired to their staterooms, Stedding would give Tillman a signal. It would be a cough—something that could be heard in the cabin, whose doors were all kept open in sultry weather. The Confederates would not recognize it as a signal, but Tillman would.[5]

As the sky grew dark on the evening of July 16, the *Waring* found itself in latitude 32° north, about forty miles east of the Gulf Stream and a hundred miles or so south of Charleston.[6] If all went as expected, it would be in Charleston's harbor the next morning. If the schooner was to be retaken, Tillman and Stedding would have to act that night, before the vessel came under the protection of Southern fortifications and guns. They could not wait.[7]

The air that hovered over the schooner that night was hot and humid, and the deck was illuminated by bright moonlight.[8] The prize captain and second mate retired to their cabin before eleven o'clock, leaving Stedding at the wheel and the first mate on the deck nearby.[9] Both Stedding and the first mate had been given orders. They were to turn the schooner to the northwest, toward Charleston, but most specifically toward the North Edisto River, a deepwater inlet that led from the coast through twisting back channels to an arm of Charleston Harbor.[10] It would be foolish to try to approach Charleston through the main harbor mouth, for Union cruisers were hovering in the sea outside, challenging any vessel that dared to run the blockade Lincoln had imposed on the coastline.[11] Approaching the harbor through one of the many inlets, coves, and backwaters that riddled the surrounding country would be much more prudent, for the Yankees could not cover all those waterways. The *Waring* would sail toward the North Edisto and elude the blockaders.

Tillman retired to his cabin stateroom at his usual hour.[12] MacKinnon went down into the cabin at about ten minutes past eleven. The Irishman was feeling a little sick when he reached his stateroom, so he poured himself a glass of brandy, drank it, slowly took off his clothes, and settled into his berth.[13]

Stedding was steering the *Waring* while the first mate was lying on the deck nearby, supposedly watching him but actually sleeping. A few minutes after MacKinnon went down into the cabin, when all aboard the schooner seemed quiet, Stedding coughed, then waited for a response. When he got none, he concluded that Tillman had not heard him and decided to go down into the cabin himself. He put the wheel in a becket (a loop of rope designed to prevent it from turning), took off his boots so he could walk across the deck without making any noise, and crept down the steps of the companionway, where he approached Tillman, who was asleep (or pretending to be asleep) in his berth.[14] Stedding moved as quietly as he could, for the doors had been taken off all the staterooms to permit the air to circulate freely, and he did not want to awaken the captain or second mate, whose berths were close by. He approached the black man, put his hand on him, and said in a whisper, "Now is our time."[15]

Tillman rose noiselessly from his berth and walked across the cabin to the place where he had hidden his hatchet six days earlier.[16] It was an innocent instrument, commonly used to perform routine tasks on the vessel, like trimming ropes, cleaning fish, or cutting wood for the cooking fires. Taking the hatchet in hand, he crossed the cabin to the prize captain's stateroom, and quickly smashed the blade into the sleeping man's skull. Twice he struck, both times with force and determination.[17]

In his berth on the other side of the cabin, MacKinnon heard a strange noise. It sounded like something striking an object—not a hard object, like a piece of wood, but something softer, like a piece of meat—and he immediately jumped up. As he did he heard another noise, this resembling the gasp or scream of a person who had somehow been attacked. It was a weak, faint kind of scream, sounding almost as if it had come from a girl about twelve years of age, but it sent a wave of terror running through the Irishman's body.[18] He looked through the open door of his stateroom and saw Tillman bounding across the cabin to the second mate's stateroom. There the steward drove his hatchet into the second mate's head, striking a kind of sideways blow. The mate tried to grasp at Tillman but could not reach him, and instead slipped out of his berth and onto the floor. MacKinnon had now gone to the door, where he looked at Tillman in stunned silence.[19] Tillman saw him and addressed him calmly. "Sir, you needn't be scared," he said. "I suppose you know what I am doing." "Yes," MacKinnon answered.[20]

Leaving the captain and second mate where they had fallen,

Tillman then climbed the companionway to the deck, where Stedding had a small pistol trained on the first mate, who had been awakened by the noise in the cabin and was rising to his feet. With a hand signal, Tillman warned the German not to fire the pistol, for the gunshot would awaken the other Confederate crewmen in their berths in the forward part of the hold and bring them topside.[21] There would be a struggle, and Tillman and Stedding would be outnumbered. Instead Tillman attacked the first mate with the same hatchet he had used on the men below. The mate fell to the deck bleeding profusely; then Tillman and Stedding dragged him to the rail and pitched his body overboard.

Tillman then returned to the cabin, where he finished his attack on the captain and second mate while the speechless MacKinnon watched. Stedding joined Tillman in the cabin, and the two men dragged the fallen bodies from the cabin up onto the deck, lifted them to the rail, and pitched them into the sea.[22] The men thrown overboard were not yet dead, for Tillman and Stedding could hear their gasps from the waves pitching below.[23]

Awakened by the commotion, the two Confederate seamen who had been asleep in their berths, James Milnor and James Dorsett, now approached the scene of the attack. Like MacKinnon, they seemed stunned. Tillman told Stedding that they would put these men into irons, saying "We have done all the butchering I guess we shall do this voyage. Those two fellows I intend to take back. There is two of them and there is two of us. I guess we can manage them pretty well without taking their lives at any rate."[24]

Tillman now took the schooner's wheel. He announced that he was in charge of the vessel and that he intended to return it to a Northern port.

The air was still hot and sultry, and the waves insistent. Tillman directed the schooner away from the North Edisto, away from the approach to Charleston and the Confederate coast, and pointed it north. He was searching for a refuge where he and Stedding would be safe from the danger of further Confederate attacks. But they could not be sure that they would reach that goal, for the distance they would have to cover was long and the perils they would encounter as they proceeded through the war-torn ocean were impossible to foresee. They had begun their voyage back to the North with bold action and for now could only pray that it would end in their freedom.[25]

FIVE

THE RETURN

It had taken only a few minutes for Tillman to attack the three officers and, with Stedding's help, throw them overboard. The *Waring* was now free of the imminent threat that it would be taken into a secessionist port and condemned, and that all the property aboard—including Tillman himself—would be sold at public auction. But the *Waring* had not been disabled by the recapture. It was still moving, still pushed forward by the winds that filled its sails and the waves that rolled under its hull. But in what direction? And with what destination? And who was now in command?

Tillman was the instigator of the recapture plot and the man who had almost single-handedly carried it out. But nobody had given him the authority to take control of the *Waring*, and the men who remained on the vessel were not sure he was the one to do so. After all, he was a lowly cook and steward, the servant of all the other men on board. He had spent years at sea, but he had always taken orders and never given them, and he had no knowledge or experience of navigation.

Maritime navigation is a demanding skill that requires the ability to ascertain the latitude and longitude of a vessel's position, how far it is from rocks, reefs, and shoals, the depth of the water beneath it, and what direction it must be pointed in to sail safely. In their looting of the *Waring*, the privateers had carried off the vessel's sextant, a handheld instrument used to calculate latitude.[1] Usually made of brass, the sextant included a frame, an arc marked in degrees, a radial arm that rotated across the arc, a telescope, and two mirrors. Held to the navigator's eye, it was used to measure the angle between the horizon and astronomical bodies such as the sun, the moon, or stars. Most sightings were taken of the sun when it is highest in the sky, which is around noon. The use of a chronometer and published tables then enabled the navigator to calculate the vessel's longitude. The privateers did leave two quadrants behind, however.[2] Quadrants were the predecessors of sextants, handheld instruments that were also used to make celestial observations, but with more difficulty and less accuracy.[3]

A maritime vessel is typically navigated by the captain and the first mate, who must have the necessary skills to take all the observations and reckonings, to make all the calculations necessary to accurately locate the vessel as it passes through a vast ocean, and to note those locations in the logbook.[4] The first mate is required to have navigational skills because he might have to take over the vessel in the event of the captain's disability or death.[5] None of the men aboard the *Waring* after its recapture had the ability to do these things.[6]

While Tillman was the first to take the wheel after the prize officers were thrown overboard, Stedding soon took his turn

steering the vessel. It was essential to determine promptly if
the two privateers who remained belowdecks, and the Scot-
tish sailor who had declined to help Tillman and Stedding
recapture the vessel, would resist the takeover. Aroused by the
commotion on deck, James Milnor, the seaman from South
Carolina, and James Dorsett, the deckhand from New Jersey,
were the first to come topside. Tillman ordered Milnor to go
down into the cabin, and as he did, Stedding saw that he was
armed with a knife. He promptly seized it and, with Tillman's
help, clapped the South Carolinian into irons. Then Stedding
went forward, where he encountered Dorsett. The New Jersey
man begged for his life but was told that he would be safe and
well treated if he would help Tillman and Stedding work the
vessel into a Northern port. Dorsett was overjoyed. Referring
to the privateers Tillman had killed, he said, "It served them
right."[7] For the time being, however, Dorsett, too, was put
in irons.

Next Tillman and Stedding called Donald McLeod out of
his berth. When the Scot came up on the deck they asked him
if he knew that they had taken the vessel. "No," McLeod said
defiantly. "I don't know anything about it." Tillman asked him
if he would help them take the vessel back to safety. "I am
going back if I can," the steward continued, "and I am going
to save the vessel & cargo if I can. We have saved ourselves so
far. I don't intend to be taken again. Before I would be taken
again I would sink this vessel and go to the bottom, scuttle
her." Impressed by Tillman's vehemence, McLeod said he

would do all he could to help get the vessel back. The steward replied curtly: "A man that won't fight has got to work."[8]

Tillman and Stedding now hove the vessel around and set it on a new course. Tillman later recalled that it was north by west while Bryce MacKinnon remembered that it was north by northeast.[9] In either case they were heading away from the dreaded Southern ports the privateers had been steering for. As the men gathered on the half deck behind the wheel to discuss their next steps, Dorsett posed a question to the steward. The lowly black man had been giving the orders, and it seemed that he was the man in charge, so the privateer from New Jersey sensed that he was the one to answer questions. "Who is the captain?" Dorsett asked. Gesturing toward Stedding, Tillman said, "Bill here is captain." He then added that McLeod would be the mate. Unpersuaded, Dorsett then asked the steward if he himself would be the captain. Tillman answered that he wouldn't. He would be "the same as he was before." MacKinnon later recalled that the men stayed up all night discussing the question Dorsett had posed.[10] But they came to no conclusions. Was it really necessary to make formal appointments? They all understood that Tillman was the man in charge.[11] He was the man who was determined that he would never be made a slave. And it was clear that they would follow his instructions.

If they could not decide who would be their master, they did agree on one essential point: If any privateer came across them again, they would either run the *Waring* ashore or, if they could not do that, abandon the vessel in a boat or drown themselves in the sea. They knew that if privateers again came aboard and saw the cabin strewn with bloody debris, they would be doomed. And if the evidence of what had happened wasn't enough, the two remaining privateers would certainly tell them. "We would be sent immediately up to the peak," MacKinnon recalled. "Up to the peak" may have referred to the practice of ordering a man to climb to the top of the highest mast ("the peak") and remain there until, exhausted, he dropped to the deck in a mass of broken bones or, worse yet, fell into the sea.[12] Or it may simply have referred to a shipboard hanging. In either case the men left on the *Waring* knew that if they ever fell into Confederate hands, they would face certain death. "We preferred drowning before that," MacKinnon said.[13]

The first night after the recapture, a mood of apprehension hovered over the *Waring*. If any of the men aboard were able to sleep, they could do so only in fits and starts, trying valiantly to rest their bodies and minds while keeping their eyes half open to the dangers that surrounded them.

The next morning Tillman came to MacKinnon. "We must now form watches," he said, "so as to protect ourselves and the vessel against the other two of the prize crew."[14] Watches may have been necessary for protection against Milnor and Dorsett—they were, after all, prisoners aboard the *Waring*—but they were also essential to guard against undetected perils that might await them in the open sea. It was habitual for the crews of sailing ships to be divided into separate divisions (watches) with clearly assigned duties and specific times when those duties were to be performed.[15]

Tillman decided that the irons could be removed from Milnor and Dorsett in return for their promises to work the ship with the other men. He then established two watches of four hours each. With only two watches, each man would be on watch three times in every twenty-four hours. Tillman and Stedding headed up the watches.[16] MacKinnon formed part of Stedding's watch with Milnor.[17]

All the men aboard the *Waring* knew that they would have to do their best to help get the schooner back to safety. There were only six of them now—barely enough to keep the vessel afloat and on course—and the duties they had to perform were the same as those required on any similar vessel. The wind had to be constantly watched, the waves and the tides carefully observed. The ship's spars and sails had to be adjusted. Yards had to be trimmed, sails furled and unfurled, rigging tightened or loosened. The wheel had to be manned, turned when necessary to change course, and kept steadily on that course until another change was called for. And the vessel had to be almost constantly pumped of the water that seeped into the hull.

Pumping was not unusual. Sailing ships were built of wood. Wood warps and twists and cracks. The planks that cover the hull shrink and expand and separate. Worms attach themselves to the planks and bore through the fibers, seeking nourishment as well as refuge from the pounding waves. The seawater relentlessly penetrates any opening that can accommodate it, and if it is not promptly removed, the vessel will sink deeper and deeper into the ocean. And rains add to the problem. At least once during the voyage north, the *Waring* was pummeled by a heavy downpour. The rain accumulated on the deck. Some ran off into the ocean, but some penetrated through the deck planks and seeped deep into the bilge. For all these reasons the vessel had to be pumped at least once every two hours. Sometimes the pumping operation took a half hour to complete; sometimes it was over in only ten minutes.[18] In either case the pumps always had to be ready, and the men on their watches available to man them.

All these duties were demanding. They required strength, a measure of intelligence, and, most important, attention—for the slightest error committed at a crucial moment could subject the vessel to untold perils.

Tillman continued to operate the galley and cook for the other men. It was a duty he was peculiarly suited for—it had after all been his occupation for years—and he performed it without complaint. Two or three times Dorsett filled in for him, but for all the rest of the time the black cook and steward prepared the food and served the meals that gave the other men the strength and energy they needed to work the vessel.[19] And although he did this faithfully, he also took his regular turns at the wheel, kept his watches, and supervised the other men on board the vessel.

As days passed, Tillman never let his guard down to the potential dangers posed by Milnor and Dorsett, or to the action he would have to take if privateers again appeared on the horizon. It was Stedding and MacKinnon's duty to keep an eye on Milnor at all times. They did not want to give the South Carolinian any opportunity to creep up behind them and try to seize the vessel yet again. Tillman watched McLeod and Dorsett. Though they had promised to help work the vessel north, the steward couldn't be sure they would keep their word.[20]

When the *Jeff Davis* looted the *Waring*, its men took all the guns they could find. They missed an old musket, however, and did not know there were two small pistols hidden aboard. Stedding had one, which he willingly turned over to Tillman, and MacKinnon another, concealed in his trunk. On the first morning after the recapture, the Irishman attempted to load his weapon with some balls and powder he had brought with him. Tillman saw what he was doing and suggested that the two men should try to fire their weapons, to determine in advance if they would work should there be any real need. Tillman loaded Stedding's pistol with a cap and a slug and attempted to fire it. The cap discharged, but the slug did not leave the barrel. He then put on several caps and again tried to make the charge go out, but it did not.[21] MacKinnon's pistol also failed to fire. The failure of the pistols was troubling. If Tillman, Stedding, and MacKinnon were ever forced into combat, they could not count on guns to help them.

It was the middle of July 1861, and the war between the United States and the self-declared Confederate States of America was in its infancy, but there was no doubt that the sea would soon become a major venue of the conflict. President Jefferson Davis had given official recognition to the importance of the sea when he invited applications for letters of marque and reprisal, and Lincoln affirmed that recognition when he proclaimed the blockade. The Union was already taking steps to strengthen its naval presence along the Southern coast.

At the same time, Louis Coxetter's *Jeff Davis* was continuing its ocean voyage, prowling the waves as far north as the Narragansett Shoals off Rhode Island for suitable vessels to add to its growing roster of prizes. On Tuesday, July 9, two days after it captured the *Waring*, it seized the ship *Mary Goodell* of Searsport, Maine, taking off water and provisions and searching for any gold and silver that might be aboard. (There had been reports that it was carrying specie.) But they found none. When the privateers realized that the *Goodell* had too deep a draft to enter any of their ports safely, they decided not to make it a prize, choosing instead to release it in return for the Yankee captain's promise to continue on his voyage to Buenos Aires. They also put twelve of the prisoners they had taken from their prizes onto the *Goodell*, including officers from the *John Welsh*, the *Enchantress*, and the *S. J. Waring*.[22] The *Davis* was already crowded with prisoners, and they did not want to be burdened with these men as they continued their privateering ventures. As soon as the *Davis* was out of view, however, the captain of the *Goodell* reversed direction and beat a hasty retreat to Portland, where the *Waring*'s captain, Frank Smith; first mate, Timothy Smith and second mate, Charles Davidson, were released.[23]

While the *Davis* was dealing with the *Goodell*, another

enticing prize from Searsport came into view. This was the brig *Mary E. Thompson*, which was carrying a cargo of lumber bound for the island of Antigua in the Caribbean. But neither the brig nor the lumber were deemed valuable enough to take as prizes, so the *Thompson*, like the *Goodell*, was sent on its way.[24]

On Friday, July 12, U.S. Secretary of the Navy Gideon Welles received a telegram advising him that the *Jeff Davis* had been spotted one hundred miles south of Nantucket.[25] That same day the commandant of the U.S. Navy Yard in Boston ordered the U.S. sloop of war *Vincennes* to pursue the marauder, and the revenue cutters *Morris* and *Caleb Cushing* joined in the effort.[26] The following Monday the *New York Herald* advised its readers that "the depredations of the Southern privateers are becoming each day more destructive and more bold."[27] Six days later the *Davis* appeared farther south, where it seized a Boston-based bark called the *Alvarado* that was loaded with a rich cargo of wool, buchu leaves (originally from Africa and valued for their medicinal properties), sheepskins, hides, and a quantity of old copper and iron. Coxetter and Postell were glad to take this cargo, for they reckoned it was worth in the neighborhood of seventy-five thousand dollars. They installed a prize crew on the *Alvarado*, as they had on the *Waring*, with orders to take it to Fernandina, Florida. As the *Alvarado* approached its destination, however, it encountered a U.S. Navy sloop of war blocking the entrance to the harbor. The prize captain panicked, ran the *Alvarado* onto a nearby shoal, and abandoned it. A boat sent out from the navy sloop was able to dodge gunfire from a nearby Confederate battery, put navy men aboard the *Alvarado*, set it afire, and destroy it.[28]

If the seawaters were hazardous for privateers and their captures, they were equally so for the *Waring* as it struggled to sail north. The men who were working the schooner knew that if it came in too close to the shoreline, it might run aground and have to be abandoned. The valuable vessel and all of its cargo would be totally lost. Even worse, Tillman and Stedding would fall into the hands of the authorities they had so boldly defied when they recaptured the vessel. Tillman had attacked the three Confederates on the schooner because he was determined never to be made a slave. Now he had to fear an even worse fate: death at the end of a hangman's noose.

The Southern coastline presented hazards even to conventional navigators. All the way from the mouth of Chesapeake Bay, the gateway to the harbors of Virginia and Maryland (and, not incidentally, the District of Columbia), to the tip of Florida, the coast was flat and low. A ridge of sand, broken here and there by occasional rivers and channels, extended its whole length. In many places the sand stretched far out into the ocean, where it formed bars and shoals on which the waves crashed relentlessly. In other places it raised islands or chains of islands that enclosed coves and sounds. Many of the shoals were covered with water at high tide and thus hidden from visual observation. The waves were constantly at work, forming islands and sandbars, carving out new channels and inlets.[29]

Lighthouses (erected by the U.S. government) stood at hazardous points along the coast, sending beams of light into the sea to help navigators avoid the treacherous shoreline. When the night air was clear, the beams could be seen for several miles by the naked eye. But when fogs crept over the coastline, as they often did, they were obscured so effectively that they were almost invisible until they suddenly appeared in the water ahead of the vessel. By that time, the shore and all its dangers would be too close to avoid.

In peacetime, a coastal navigator could find shelter by heading for one of the many ports—some large and some small—scattered along the coastline. The men now in charge of the *Waring* could not count on any such refuges. They had to scrupulously avoid Southern harbors, for they could be taken prisoner there. If the *Waring* foundered on the coastline, they would be left to their own devices to try to save themselves from the secessionist authorities who now regarded them not only as enemies but also as criminals.

The years Tillman had spent aboard merchant vessels plying the Southern coast had acquainted him with many of its landmarks. He had been on deck for much of that time, observing shoals, islands, channels, rivers, forests, and lighthouses. He recognized many of the landmarks on sight. But in his present situation he did not want to come so close to the coast that he could recognize these features. He needed to stay well away from the perils that the land posed to him and the ship he was struggling to bring back to a Northern port. There were books and charts in the captain's cabin—left there when Captain Smith was taken off the *Waring* by the privateers. But they were of little use to the black steward who was now in charge of the *Waring*, for he could not read or even write his own name. When it was necessary for him to sign a document, he could only make a cross or X.[30] This was a common kind of personal affirmation in an era in which so many men and women, whites as well as blacks, were completely illiterate. Stedding was almost as illiterate as Tillman. In the court testimony he gave after his return to New York, the German stated that he could not read or write English—suggesting perhaps that he was not illiterate in his native language.[31] McLeod told the court in New York that he was unable either to read or write.[32]

Bryce MacKinnon, however, was an educated man, able to read and write the English language, and thus able to help Tillman and Stedding. He rummaged through the papers, books, and charts left in the captain's cabin and found there a copy of the *American Coast Pilot*, a large, heavy volume published by the firm of Edmund and George W. Blunt and popularly known as *Blunt's Coast Pilot*. More than seven hundred pages long and printed in small type, with charts added for visual clarification, the *Coast Pilot* was almost universally used by navigators along the Atlantic Coast. Originally published in Newburyport, Massachusetts, in 1796, it had moved to New York with its many subsequent editions. It described the principal harbors, capes, and headlands of the coasts of both North and South America, including directions for navigators, soundings, and bearings of lighthouses and beacons. It included information about prevailing winds, currents, and the latitudes and longitudes of the principal harbors and capes, together with a table of all the tides that navigators could encounter.[33] It was an indispensable resource for professional navigators, although its usefulness to Tillman was questionable: It was necessary to sight many landmarks before consulting their descriptions in the *Coast Pilot*, and it was often necessary to take reckonings and make observations to determine latitudes and longitudes.

MacKinnon made use of his writing ability by sitting down in the *Waring*'s cabin when he was not on watch or performing other duties and writing an account of the events that had taken place on the vessel since it was recaptured from the privateers. He naturally hoped that he would one day make it back to New York, and when he got there he wanted to remember clearly what had happened and to communicate his recollection to the authorities. He began writing his account on the first day after the recapture and continued it every day thereafter.[34]

From the moment he took charge of the *Waring*, it was evident that Tillman had a good sense of the course the vessel should set. MacKinnon later recalled that the men aboard never argued about their direction. When anybody stated an opinion regarding it, the others seemed to agree.[35] Inevitably it was Tillman who most often expressed his opinions, for, whatever his limitations, the black man had more experience sailing along the Southern coast than any of the others. During the first night after the recapture, Tillman set a course for north by west, determining his direction with the use of the *Waring*'s compass. His choice of a slightly westerly direction probably reflected his sense that the *Waring* was far enough east of the coastline to ensure its safety. On the first morning after the recapture, Wednesday, July 17, he and Stedding altered the course to a more northerly direction. North Carolina was to their west now, and the Gulf Stream, which impeded the southward voyages of coastal vessels, was helping them move north. On Thursday, July 18, they again steered north by west. Fog lay over the coastline, and Tillman determined that it was necessary to take soundings to find out the depth of the water and determine if there was any danger from shoals. He asked MacKinnon to check the *Coast Pilot* to see "if he could find any soundings of the Bodie Island shoals."[36]

Bodie Island forms a part of the treacherous Outer Banks of North Carolina, a chain of sandy islands enclosing large inland sounds. The islands are long and low, but they still help to guard the mainland from some of the treacherous storms and frequent fogs that plague the coastline. Bodie is scarcely thirty miles north of Cape Hatteras, the most easterly protrusion of the coastline anywhere south of Delaware, and a notorious peril to coastal shipping. Because of the many ships that had foundered on Hatteras, the cape and its surrounding area had for centuries been known as the "Graveyard of the Atlantic." By seeking a point along the shore north of Hatteras, Tillman was trying to avoid the hazards of the cape.

Built in 1802, the lighthouse on Bodie Island rose sixty-five feet above sea level and was equipped with a Fresnel lens* that sent alternating red and white flashes into the ocean.[37] Mac-Kinnon read aloud from the *Coast Pilot*, giving Tillman the soundings that could be expected off Bodie Island. Tillman then took his own soundings, lowering ropes into the water to determine its depth. His soundings did not match the depths recorded in the *Coast Pilot*, so he knew he was not off Bodie. He continued north.

The *Waring* was moving rapidly now. It passed the mouth of Chesapeake Bay, the gateway to Norfolk and the Gosport Navy Yard and site of many of the Confederacy's most recent naval efforts. It was also the locale of the Union navy's heaviest blockading efforts. But the *Waring* was not molested by any vessels.

After about an hour of sailing, the schooner approached a sandbar called Winter Shoals. Located about six and a half miles off the coast of Assateague, a long, sandy island that guards the Virginia coast above the Chesapeake, Winter Shoals was a notoriously treacherous location. The *Coast Pilot* described it as "a highly dangerous shoal, as the soundings change suddenly, and it lies directly in the track of vessels. The sea breaks upon it in heavy weather."[38] But a prominent lighthouse rose from the southeast corner of neighboring Chinco-

---

*Named for Augustin-Jean Fresnel, the French nineteenth-century physicist whose groundbreaking work in optics made modern lighthouses possible.

teague Island. It was equipped with a fixed light that rose eighty feet above sea level. According to the *Coast Pilot*: "This light can be seen about 12 miles in clear weather."[39]

As the *Waring* approached, the men on board began to take soundings. MacKinnon later recalled that it was Stedding who first suggested that they do so but that it was Tillman who pitched the leads into the water. Soap was attached to the ends of the leads, which enabled them to pick up fragments of sand, rocks, and shells from the ocean floor. MacKinnon read from the *Coast Pilot* when the soundings were taken, helping Tillman and Stedding determine their location, which turned out to be well north of Chesapeake Bay.[40]

They passed the mouth of Delaware Bay, probably not much more than thirty miles from Tillman's birthplace, but made no effort to enter. Delaware was still a slave state and, although it had not joined the Confederacy, many of its residents supported the Southern secessionists. Tillman had left Delaware eleven years earlier and had no friends there he could count on to help him if they made landfall.

Before long they were north of Cape May, the point of land that guards the northern entrance to Delaware Bay, and sailing along the coast of New Jersey, the first free state they had seen since they ousted the Confederates from the schooner. They must have felt a sense of exultation, knowing that much of their hazardous voyage was behind them and that their home port was not far away. But their voyage was not yet over. The sea-lanes opposite the New Jersey shore remained dangerous, for Confederate privateers still prowled the northern

Atlantic and could swoop down on the *Waring* at almost any moment, ready to retake it as a prize.

On Saturday, July 20, at about ten o'clock at night, they passed Barnegat Inlet, the narrow channel leading through a long barrier island that separates Barnegat Bay from the crashing waves along the outer shore.[41] According to the *Coast Pilot*, a shoal extended from Barnegat for two miles into the sea, and it was not prudent to approach the inlet at night in less than nine or ten fathoms of water. But a lighthouse with a flashing beacon on the south side of the inlet served to warn vessels to steer clear of the hazards.[42] Tillman saw the lighthouse, but he had no intention of heading into Barnegat. His goal now was some sixty miles distant. It was Sandy Hook, the peninsula that protrudes from the northeast corner of the New Jersey shore and marks the entrance to New York Harbor.[43]

The *Waring* sailed all night long, overshooting Sandy Hook and coming up on the morning of Sunday, July 21, off the southern shore of Fire Island, the thin barrier island that separates Long Island from the Atlantic. Pilot boats were prowling the sea all around New York City, looking for vessels they could bring into the harbor. Almost always hired to bring sailing ships into harbors, pilots knew the local waters better than any of the ship navigators and could avoid dangers that were not readily apparent: perilously shallow waters, rocks hiding just beneath the surface, shoals, treacherous currents, and similar hazards.

By nine o'clock the men aboard the *Waring* had taken on a pilot named Charles E. Warner. His boat was the *Jane*.[44] They also hired a steam-powered tug that could tow them through the Narrows, for the currents there are strong, and if the tide is flowing out, it can be difficult if not impossible to sail against them powered only by the wind.[45]

By four o'clock in the afternoon they dropped anchor off the Battery.[46] Five harrowing days had passed since William Tillman took the *Waring* back from the privateers; seventeen days had elapsed since the schooner left New York on its intended voyage to South America. Tillman and Stedding were wonderfully relieved, for they had accomplished an almost impossible feat, one that none of the men on board had any confidence they would achieve when they began their effort.

McLeod and MacKinnon shared Tillman's and Stedding's relief, although probably not as intensely, for they had never been in as much danger as the black steward and the German seaman. The Confederate prisoners, Dorsett and Milnor, in contrast, must have felt a sense of apprehension. They had avoided the fate suffered by the prize officers—they were still alive. But how would they be dealt with when they were brought ashore? Would they be greeted as free men, or would they be clapped into irons and charged with crimes—possibly even the most serious crime of all, treason, for which the penalty was hanging?

New York Harbor was quiet now, for it was Sunday afternoon and the city was at rest. But the quiet was a preliminary only to a great burst of noise, confusion, and enthusiasm that would soon follow.

SIX

A HERO'S WELCOME

While the *Waring* lay at anchor, several small boats came out to meet it. One was the news boat used by the Associated Press to pool reporters' stories from incoming ships and distribute them to the city's newspapers. Another was the New York Harbor Police boat. The police boarded the schooner first, ordering the reporters to remain in their boat while the police made their inquiries. Interest in what had happened aboard the *Waring* was intense. Some reports had trickled into New York about its capture by the *Jeff Davis*. Capt. Frank Smith, who had been transferred to the *Mary Goodell* from the *Davis*, had made it back to Portland, Maine, where he told how the privateers had captured the *Waring*, and news of that event had been telegraphed to newspapers in other cities.[1] But the story of the schooner's recapture from the privateers wasn't known.

The police officers peppered Tillman with questions, and he answered them freely. MacKinnon did the same, even providing the officers with his written account of what had happened aboard the *Waring* after the privateers seized it. The police went into the cabin where Tillman had attacked

Montague Amiel and George Stephens with his hatchet. There they found bloody clothes and bedding, mute testimony to the awful scene that had played out there. MacKinnon said that a "pail full" of blood must have come from the two men. In the cabin they also found the remnants of the American flag that the privateers had cut up to produce their rebel banner. They were shown the hatchet that Tillman used in the attack. It appeared to be an ordinary one, the kind kept for chopping wood, not one designed to be used as a weapon.[2]

The police took all the men off the *Waring* and transported them to their headquarters on State Street, where a crowd had assembled.[3] Then they were turned over to the U.S. marshal, Robert Murray. If crimes had been committed while the *Waring* was at sea, the marshal and the U.S. courts would have jurisdiction to determine guilt or innocence and impose whatever penalties the law required. From police headquarters, the men were taken to the House of Detention on White Street, where further inquiries were made. The marshal quickly came to the conclusion that Dorsett and Milnor would have to be jailed, for they were rebel privateers, but that the other men only had to be detained for questioning.[4] Tillman's interrogation included at least one session before the federal grand jury.[5]

It was becoming clear that Tillman was the man responsible for recapturing the *Waring*, that he had almost single-handedly killed the three prize officers aboard the schooner, turned it around, and brought it back to New York. On Monday the authorities continued their investigations while the people of the city buzzed with excitement about details of the story that were then leaking out. On Tuesday morning a group of officers, reporters, and ordinary citizens gathered in the marshal's office, where Tillman was the focus of attention. The *Herald* said that he was greeted by all with the "warmest expressions of esteem and laudation for the manner in which he had taken from the robber hands of the rebels the property so ruthlessly stolen."[6]

Tillman was seated in an armchair as the room began to fill. As each person approached him, he rose and bowed. He conversed with what the *Herald* called "much care and affability," and he did not hesitate to answer any question that was put to him.[7]

"I am glad to see you," said one man. "You deserve to have your liberty."

"Yes," said another, "if all the colored people were like you, we would not have all this trouble."

"I did the best I could," Tillman replied. "I couldn't see any other way to get my liberty."

The incident aboard the *Waring* that most "incensed" the black man was the tearing up of the Stars and Stripes in order to make a rebel flag of it. "This made my blood boil," Tillman said, "and I vowed to have revenge." Tillman then recalled statements made by the privateers that revealed they were intending to make him a slave. "When the captain of the privateer came on board, he told me that he would yet see me down in Savannah, and there he would deal with me as he pleased. I said to myself, 'Old man, you will never catch me down there.'"[8]

A man asked Tillman how he felt after "slaying the three men, and throwing them overboard."

"I felt as though I had done a good action," Tillman answered, "and done service to that Union which I love."

"God will bless you for your deed, my friend," the man answered.

"I hope so, sir. I am sure I would not have taken the lives of these men if I could have avoided it, but it was utterly impossible to regain the schooner without sacrificing their lives."

"Were the men whom you killed stout, muscular men?" one questioner asked.

"They were, the captain in particular. He was a strong, able-bodied man, and seemed to possess a vast amount of natural strength."

"Did you have much difficulty in mastering these men?"

"None whatever. They struggled a little, but I put them overboard quicker than lightning. They all had breathing life in them, and as they sank in the sea my heart palpitated slightly. It was a feeling of sorrow that I had been compelled to sacrifice human life. Everything being as still as midnight on the sea could possibly make it, I felt a shuddering sensation; but as soon as I felt the cause which impelled me on to the deed, I felt relieved."

The marshal asked Tillman if he had been "in the habit of killing hogs."

"I never killed but one before," Tillman answered, "and that one was a pig."

Tillman said that at first he had thought of "securing all the men" and bringing them to New York in irons, but he found this was impossible. "They were too many for that. There were five of them and only three of us. After this I said, well, I will get all I can back alive, and the rest I will kill."[9]

"Do you desire anything in the way of providing you comfortably in your present quarters?" a man asked.

"I am perfectly satisfied with what has been provided for me," Tillman answered.[10]

As the questioning continued, Tillman revealed that James Dorsett had come to him six days before he recaptured the *Waring* and asked if he was "willing to shed blood in order to recover the vessel." Suspecting Dorsett's motives, Tillman said he would not do anything like that—that he had "made up his mind to take the worst." Unknown to Dorsett, Tillman had already made his plans with Stedding to retake the vessel and was just waiting for a favorable moment "to strike the blow."

The U.S. district attorney, E. Delafield Smith, then entered the room. He walked up to Tillman, saying, "I am glad to see you, sir, and shake you by the hand."

"He saved you a good deal of trouble," a nearby man commented.[11]

The district attorney laughed and then informed Tillman that he was going to be detained as a witness. He said that the law required him to hold witnesses, regardless of whether they were going to be charged with crimes. He would be detained until Dorsett and Milnor had been examined. In the meantime he could be released on bail. Several prominent New York merchants had offered to post bail for him if he wished to go at liberty.[12]

"I am perfectly willing to abide by anything you may say," Tillman answered.[13]

"We'll have to run you for president," Smith joked. The crowd laughed.

"I don't want to go quite so high as that," the black man answered.[14]

Tillman made a good impression on the people he spoke to. A reporter for the New York Tribune gave readers a physical description. He was of "medium height, rather strongly built, crisp hair, of nearly unmixed negro blood." More important, the reporter noted that he "bears in his countenance an expression of honesty, strong sense, with some touches of humor."[15]

William Stedding was also present in the marshal's office and, like Tillman, he was an object of curiosity. But he had little to say. According to the Times, he "seemed modest and retiring."[16]

The secession flag that the privateers had made out of the Stars and Stripes, which the Times said "was stained with the blood of the chief of the pirate crew," and the hatchet Tillman had used in the attack, were on hand during the questioning. The reporters and bystanders inspected them "with great interest."[17]

Leaving the marshal's office, Tillman and Stedding were led to the office of the New York Board of Underwriters on Wall Street. This was a powerful association of insurance companies organized for the purpose of cooperating in matters relating to their business. Nine of the eleven members were marine insurers, including Atlantic Mutual, Commercial Mutual, Great Western, Mercantile Mutual, New York Mutual, Oriental Mutual, Pacific Mutual, Sun Mutual, and Union Mutual. All maintained offices near the New York headquarters of the *Waring*'s owner, Jonas Smith. Samuel J. Waring, namesake of Smith's now-famous schooner, maintained his office at 51 Wall Street, the same address as Atlantic Mutual. While an early report in the *Herald* had said that there was no insurance on the *Waring*,[18] the special interest the Board of Underwriters showed in Tillman and Stedding, and the prominent role insurance companies played in the ultimate resolution of legal issues flowing from the *Waring*'s recapture, proved otherwise.

The black steward and the German seaman were invited to meet with the board to inform them of "the particulars of the recapture of the vessel." The *New York Sun* reported that Tillman "gave a succinct and lively narrative of the capture of the schooner and his manner of recapturing her." A committee of three merchants was then appointed to determine if Tillman and Stedding were entitled to salvage awards for recapturing the *Waring*.[19] "The men will no doubt receive a liberal reward for their heroic conduct," the *Sun* said.[20] The *Times* added that the underwriters expressed "the intention to reward the men handsomely, which they can well afford to do, as the value of the vessel and cargo is estimated at over $100,000." The companies "interested" were, according to the *Times*, Atlantic Mutual, Great Western, New York Commercial, Mercantile

Mutual, and the Pacific Insurance Company.[21] It seems likely from this report that these five companies were coinsurers of the *Waring*. They had shared the risks of the loss of the vessel and its cargo on its long voyage to South America and were mutually obligated to compensate the men who had recaptured the vessel from the privateers.

As soon as the major newspapers digested the facts they heard from Tillman, MacKinnon, and the other men from the *Waring*, they began to praise the black man for his courage. The pro-Republican *New York Tribune*, run by the mercurial Horace Greeley, whose opinions about the Civil War were loudly expressed and frequently changed, despite his consistent opposition to slavery and support for the Union, said that "Wm. Tillman, a colored man, is the one hero in this chapter of history." The *Herald*, run by the pro-Democratic James Gordon Bennett, a defender of slavery but a fierce foe of secession, wrote that "the prime source of this fortunate escape from the fangs of a bloodthirsty enemy is the heroism and wonderful presence of mind of a negro named William Tillman."[22] The *Herald* called Tillman "the gallant steward—the splendid son of Africa" and told its readers that his name "will now become historic as the enacter of as great a piece of daring and heroism as perhaps the world ever saw."[23]

The abolitionist press was also quick to pick up on Tillman's story and to praise his heroism. *The Liberator*, published in Boston by the most prominent of all the abolitionists, William Lloyd Garrison, extolled the "extraordinary daring and skill" with which Tillman recaptured the *Waring* from the privateers. While acknowledging that the whole event was a "tragedy," *The Liberator* maintained that Tillman's feat was "brilliant and daring" and that he was clearly "the hero of the tragedy."[24]

Around the same time, the noted black orator and writer Frederick Douglass wrote an article about Tillman's recapture of the *Waring* in *Douglass' Monthly*, the newspaper he published in Rochester, New York. "One of the most daring and heroic deeds," Douglass declared, "—one which will be likely to inflict the heaviest blow upon the piratical enterprises of *Jeff. Davis*—has been struck by an obscure negro. . . . When we consider all the circumstances of this transaction, we cannot fail to perceive in Tillman a degree of personal valor and presence of mind equal to those displayed by the boldest deeds recorded in history." Douglass noted that Tillman had acted virtually alone, and totally without the army support that most military heroes have. Tillman had "no one to share danger with him," Douglass said. He had to "draw from his own bosom the stern confidence required for the performance of the task of man-slaying. . . . The soldier knows that even in case of defeat there are stronger probabilities in his favor than against him. Tillman, on the other side, was almost alone against five, and well knew that if he failed, an excruciating death would be the consequence."[25]

Supporting Douglass, Gerrit Smith, a wealthy landowner in upstate New York who had supported John Brown's raid on Harpers Ferry and stoutly proclaimed the cause of abolitionism, wrote an open letter to Abraham Lincoln that was published in both *The Liberator* and *Douglass' Monthly*. He called the conflict that now raged between the North and South a "slavery-begotten" war and argued that "the South would never have made the War had not slavery first made her mad." Smith chided Lincoln for not calling on blacks to join the military forces he was then marshaling in the North, recalling the bravery and valor that black units had exhibited during the American War of Independence. "Among the black men who would have sprung forward in response to your call," Smith insisted, "hundreds would have exhibited as high heroism as William Tillman, the black sailor who, as yet, stands at the head of all the heroes of the present war. In response to that call, many a black man would have shown himself as eager to be early in this war, as was Crispus Attucks to be early in the Revolutionary War. For it was in one of the very first skirmishes in the dawn of the Revolution that this noble black man led a party to Boston, and sealed his patriotism with his blood."[26]

On the afternoon of Friday, August 2, a large gathering of free blacks assembled in a park in New Bedford, Massachusetts, to celebrate the twenty-seventh anniversary of the end of slavery in the British West Indies. Slavery had been promoted and protected in all the British colonies in America (including those that later joined to form the United States) for centuries before it was ended by an act of Parliament that became effective on August 1, 1834. That day was thereafter remembered in Britain as "a biblical Jubilee, a millennial turning point in human history."[27]

The celebrants in New Bedford listened to speakers who recalled the historic day of British emancipation and expressed their hopes for a similar day in the United States. At the same time, however, they turned their minds toward the more recent accomplishments of William Tillman, adopting a formal resolution that congratulated him for his "heroic act" in recapturing the schooner *Waring* and its cargo by "taking the lives of the piratical crew, thereby saving valuable property to the amount of $100,000; and also in saving what is of more value than money, his own liberty." The resolution condemned the "atrocious" act of "his un-excellency, the arch-traitor and would-be President, Jeff Davis," in authorizing the letters of marque and reprisal that had sent "piratical vessels" out to sea to prey on American ships. It declared that Tillman was "entitled to the unanimous thanks of the United States Congress" for his recapture of the *Waring*. It also authorized the appointment of three men to present the resolution to the local representative and thus to Congress itself.[28]

Congress never did thank William Tillman for his recapture of the *S. J. Waring*, nor did Abraham Lincoln acknowledge Gerrit Smith's letter praising the black steward for his heroism. But both Congress and the president would soon do much more to support the cause of black freedom in America than any previous president or Congress ever had: first by emancipating all slaves in areas of the country in rebellion against the government and, second, by amending the U.S. Constitution to wholly abolish slavery in all states of the Union, South as well as North.

Of course the praise for William Tillman in the North was not echoed in the South. One Southern newspaper condemned Tillman as "a cowardly black butcher of brave sleeping men."[29] From the time of the Haitian revolution led by Toussaint Louverture in the 1790s through John Brown's raid on Harpers Ferry, Virginia, in 1859—an attack led by a white abolitionist but supported by blacks—Southerners had dreaded and roundly condemned black violence against whites, wherever it occurred, whatever its result, and however it was provoked. And they had promptly and brutally punished it.

Not surprisingly, stories about Tillman's recapture of the *Waring* were published all over the country—in New England, in New York and Pennsylvania, in the Ohio River valley, and even in faraway California, to which reports were carried over the plains and the mountains by the Pony Express. The national press also noted Tillman's heroism, with articles published by *Harper's Weekly, Scientific American*, and *Frank Leslie's Illustrated Weekly*. The *Harper's* article was illustrated with wood engravings showing key events in Tillman's story, and an image of the *Waring* as it lay at anchor.[30] A long account of Tillman's successful recapture of the *Waring* also appeared in *The Times* of London.[31]

One of the most curious articles about Tillman appeared in the *American Phrenological Journal*, a monthly magazine of "science, literature, and general intelligence" published in New

York.[32] Phrenology was a popular pseudoscience based on the self-proclaimed belief that particular areas of the brain were responsible for such human character traits as intelligence, benevolence, destructiveness, and self-esteem, and that their strength could be determined by examining the size and shape of the skull. From its beginnings in Europe in the 1790s, phrenology was regarded as a field of legitimate scientific interest, but as its practitioners began to line their pockets with fees for skull readings, with proceeds from the sale of plaster busts showing areas of the brain associated with identifiable character traits, and with a very profitable publishing program in both England and the United States, it began to be regarded as quackery. Critics derided it as the "science of bumps" and charged that phrenologists were preying on a gullible public.[33] But by the outbreak of the Civil War the *American Phrenological Journal*, first published in 1838, still remained one of the country's most popular magazines.

Since slavery was such a divisive issue among Americans, it was inevitable that phrenologists would weigh in on it, some claiming that the size and shape of African American skulls proved the inferiority of blacks, and others declaring that African Americans were well suited by their mental qualities to live free lives, unburdened by the scourge of slavery.[34] The September 1861 issue of the journal featured studies of the phrenology of George B. McClellan, the young general Lincoln had just chosen to head up the Union armies; Elizabeth Barrett Browning, the popular English poet who had recently died; and the humble black man, William Tillman, whose "heroic conduct in recapturing the schooner *S. J. Waring*, and bringing her safely into New York, has excited great interest and attention."[35] After examining Tillman the journal reported that his "constitution is strong; he has broad shoulders, is thick set and well built, weighing, we judge, about one hundred and seventy-five pounds. His head measures twenty-two inches in circumference; and from a careful personal examination we find the following developments":

> He has more than a common degree of Firmness and self-reliance, considerable Self-Esteem, and large Approbativeness and Conscientiousness. His social faculties are well indicated. His Combativeness and Destructiveness are not predominant qualities, though they are rather strong. We judge that he would never quarrel nor exercise cruelty if he could well avoid it, but that he would be executive and thorough in whatever he undertook to do. The organs which give perseverance, self-reliance, sense of justice, and courage are strong. . . . He is pleasant in his manners and speech, and appears to be possessed of a kindly disposition; but his great resolution and determination, acted upon by the sense of self-preservation, made him brave and heroic in his late trying circumstances; and we fancy that we discovered a shade of sadness on his countenance, as if these fifteen days of peril had left their mark.[36]

A hint of racism surfaced when the article described Tillman as "shrewder than the general run of his race," but this was largely erased by the magazine's full account of the black man's heroics aboard the *Waring* and by its comment that he "saw slavery staring him in the face, and he undertook the bold step, which was attended with success."[37]

There had been many military skirmishes between Northern and Southern forces in the weeks following the fall of Fort Sumter. Most took place in northern Virginia, but others centered in the Shenandoah Valley, in the Kanawha Valley of western Virginia, and in much more distant locations in Missouri, Arkansas, and even Texas.

One of the most dramatic such events took place in late May after federal troops crossed the Potomac and, without armed opposition, occupied Alexandria, Virginia. Their purpose there was to seize high ground that the Confederates could use to rain artillery fire down on Washington. In the lead of the occupying troops were the Eleventh New York Fire Zouaves, commanded by the twenty-four-year-old Elmer Ellsworth. Colonel Ellsworth had popularized the uniforms of baggy pants, short jackets, and fezzes worn by French colonial troops (or Zouaves) in North Africa. He was a kind of surrogate son of Abraham Lincoln, for he had worked in Lincoln's law office in Springfield, Illinois, before accompanying the president-elect to Washington in February 1861, and later going to New York to raise a regiment to join the Union war effort. In Alexandria, Ellsworth saw a Confederate flag flying atop a hotel. It was in so prominent a location that it could be seen from the White House across the river. He climbed the stairs to the top of the hotel to remove it, and as he came down with the banner in hand he was confronted by the hotel proprietor, who leveled a shotgun at him and fired at point-blank range. Ellsworth was killed instantly. The proprietor in turn was quickly killed by one of Ellsworth's men. The young colonel's body was taken to the White House, where it lay in state as Lincoln and the people of the North grieved his loss. Lincoln called Ellsworth's death a "murder."[38] In reply to a congressman who claimed to find solace in the fact that the Stars and Stripes now flew over the Alexandria hotel, the president said: "Yes, but it was at a terrible cost!"[39] Some regarded Elmer Ellsworth as the first Northern hero of the war, but because his bravery ended in death, many Northerners preferred to call him the "first martyr" instead.[40]

Although some of the military conflicts in the early weeks of the war had been costly (there were some deaths and many injuries), none had been major encounters. The North continued to build up its military forces, while the South assembled militiamen under the command of Brigadier General Beauregard, the successful commander in the attack on Fort Sumter, and Brig. Gen. Joseph E. Johnston. Both sides, however, were growing impatient for a decisive battle.

In June, Confederate forces began to assemble around an important railroad center at Manassas, Virginia, about twenty-nine miles southwest of Washington, and as they did so North-

erners began to call for action. Lt. Gen. Winfield Scott, Lincoln's
commanding general, had counseled a slow but steady campaign
to establish federal military control of the Mississippi River.
Combined with the Union blockade of the Confederate coast,
Scott said that this would effectively surround the Confederacy and prod loyal Unionists in the secessionist states to bring
down Jefferson Davis's government. Commentators labeled
Scott's proposal the "Anaconda Plan" (for the eponymous snake
that kills its prey by coiling around and crushing it), noting
that if it was successful it would "squeeze the South to military
death." But it would take a long time to effectuate fully, and both
Northerners and Southerners were eager for a more immediate
confrontation.[41]

Lincoln sent Brig. Gen. Irvin McDowell and thirty-five
thousand troops south to challenge the Confederate troops
massing under Beauregard. Unknown to McDowell, however,
Beauregard's twenty-two thousand troops were being supple-
mented by twelve thousand additional soldiers from the northern Shenandoah Valley under Johnston. The men on both sides
were inexperienced in major fighting and poorly trained. But
one of the commanders in Johnston's force was a former professor from the Virginia Military Institute recently appointed
to the rank of brigadier general under Johnston. He was
Thomas Jonathan Jackson, soon to be acclaimed as Stonewall
Jackson after another officer watched him in battle and report-
edly exclaimed, "There is Jackson standing like a stone wall."[42]

Fighting broke out along Bull Run, a sluggish river running
north and east of Manassas, at dawn on the morning on Sun-

day, July 21, the same day that the *Waring* sailed back into
New York Harbor. The combat continued nearly the whole
day, with the Union forces sometimes gaining the initiative
and the Confederates at other times demonstrating superior strategy and execution. Confederate president Jefferson
Davis managed to leave his new capital at Richmond in time
to witness the closing moments of the battle. When he saw
the Union troops fleeing in panic, he was jubilant and urged
his generals to continue on to Washington. But they were too
disorganized to do so. As the Northern soldiers fled the field
of combat, they encountered spectators who had come out to
watch their expected victory and were appalled to see the fear
in the soldiers' faces.

When the news of the Union army's rout reached Southern
leaders, they shouted their glee. Confederate congressman–
turned–military commander Thomas R. Cobb of Georgia
announced his conviction that the victory at Bull Run (called
Manassas in the South) was "one of the decisive battles of
the world," while the writer, editor, agriculturist, and fervent secessionist Edmund Ruffin described it as "virtually the
close of the war."[43] Meanwhile a pall of gloom settled over the
North. The New York lawyer and diarist George Templeton
Strong wrote: "Today will be known as BLACK MONDAY.
We are utterly and disgracefully routed, beaten, whipped."
The *New York Tribune*'s Horace Greeley wrote Lincoln: "The
gloom in this city is funereal for our dead at Bull Run were
many, and they lie unburied yet. On every brow sits sullen,
scorching, black despair."[44]

July 21 had indeed been a bloody day at Bull Run. About 387 Confederates and 460 Union soldiers had been killed. The total of the wounded on both sides was more than 2,500.[45] Comparing the deaths suffered at Bull Run with the deaths sustained when Tillman recaptured the *S. J. Waring*, and measuring them against the results achieved in the two events, it was easy to see why so many acclaimed Tillman's action as a Union victory and bemoaned Bull Run as a Union tragedy.

As soon as the U.S. district attorney, E. Delafield Smith, concluded his examinations of Tillman and Stedding, he told them that they were free to go and that he did not plan to file any criminal charges against them. As they walked out on the streets of New York, they were thronged by hundreds of curious men and women. Some were eager to shake their hands and congratulate them for their heroic recapture of the *Waring*. Some were merely content to observe them from a distance. Yet others were hostile, regarding them (or at least Tillman, who had killed the three privateers on the *Waring*) as villains if not vicious murderers.

There was, however, one man in New York who probably didn't care much whether Tillman and Stedding were heroes or villains but who realized that money could be made from them and was confident that he was the one to do so. He was the fifty-one-year-old Phineas T. Barnum, legendary entrepreneur, showman, and proprietor of the most popular entertainment venue in the city, Barnum's American Museum on lower Broadway. Barnum's museum was a looming, five-story pile of bricks faced on the outside with gleaming marble, ornamented with colorful paintings and banners, and crowned on its roof with a Drummond light that showered brilliant limelight all over the area.[46] Inside it was filled with odd exhibits, stuffed animals, South Sea specimens, and "lecture rooms" in which celebrities could entertain large audiences.

Barnum had never been shy about employing controversial people to perform, or merely "exhibit" themselves, in his museum. He was frank to admit that his principal goal in life was making money, and for a quarter of a century he had done that by showcasing an odd collection of freaks, frauds, and genuinely notable performers to crowds of enthusiastic audiences.[47]

Barnum's views about black people had not been very favorable when he began his career as a showman. His first sensational act was a superannuated black woman named Joice Heth, who was advertised as the childhood nurse to George Washington and whose age was claimed to be 161 years. Barnum knew from the start that the black woman was not nearly as old as his advertising posters claimed, a fact that was proved in 1836, when Heth died and a physician conducting an autopsy determined that she was no more than 80 years old.[48] His promotion of her, like his promotion of hundreds of other "curiosities"—bearded ladies, towering giants, tiny dwarfs, animals imported from Asia and Africa, and even the "mummified remains of a mermaid"—was, if not blatantly fraudulent, at least grossly exaggerated. He said that the titles that had made him famous—"humbug" and "Prince of Humbugs"—were first applied to him by himself, and he proudly wrote: "I made these titles a part of my 'stock in trade.' "[49] But he also brought serious performers to his stage—the vivacious Austrian ballerina Fanny Elssler and the great Swedish soprano Jenny Lind among them.

Barnum advertised his acts lavishly, and one of his favorite strategies was to plant the seeds of doubt in the public about his most outlandish claims and challenge people to come to his museum and decide for themselves whether the claims were true or false. Had Joice Heth really been George Washington's nurse? Were the "mummified remains" he had on display really those of a mermaid? When the people came, of course, they paid admission fees and filled Barnum's pockets handsomely.

Barnum had once been a supporter of slavery. On one of his extended tours through the South in the late 1830s, he purchased a slave to serve as his valet and whipped him when he suspected him of thievery, and he accepted a slave woman and her child as partial payment for a steamboat he sold.[50] In politics he was an enthusiastic supporter of President Andrew Jackson, a slaveholder, and of Jackson's proslavery party, the Democrats.[51] Reflecting the racism that was prevalent in New York (and in many of the other Northern states as well), he restricted the admission of blacks to his museum to specified times. In an advertisement published in the *New York Tribune* in 1849, for example, he posted a "notice to persons of color" that read:

In order to afford respectable colored persons an opportunity to witness the extraordinary attractions at present
exhibited at the Museum, the Manager has determined
to admit this class of people on Thursday morning next,
March 1, from 8 A.M. till 1 P.M. Special performances in
the Lecture Room at 11 o'clock.[52]

Many blacks were happy to be told that they were welcome
in Barnum's museum, if only at specified times and only if they
were "respectable." All others could expect to be turned away.

By the 1850s, however, Barnum's enthusiasm for both slavery and the Democrats had waned. He had learned a good deal
about the cruelty that slaves were subject to and was appalled
by it; but he was also troubled by the Democratic Party's support of the Kansas-Nebraska Act of 1854, which sanctioned
the spread of slavery into the western territories if voters in
those territories (all white men, of course) chose to permit it.
By 1860 he had become an enthusiastic supporter of Lincoln
and the Republicans as well as a strong opponent of slavery.[53]

On July 25, 1861, the *New York Times* reported that Tillman and Stedding had visited Barnum's museum the previous day. As soon as it became known that they were in the
museum, the *Times* said, "they were surrounded by a large
crowd of the visitors present, and at once found themselves
the lions of the occasion, and apparently the chief attraction
of the place." The crowd was anxious to hear the particulars
of their encounter "with the pirates" and called on them to
repeat their stories over and over again. They were so busy

answering questions that they had "no time to inspect the curiosities which they came to see" and asked Barnum to allow them to come back the next day without further admission charges. Barnum assured them they could come back as often as they pleased. The *Times* reported that the "large numbers of people who have applied for permission to see them at the house for the detention of witnesses will, therefore, have an opportunity of gratifying their curiosity by visiting the Museum on any day during the coming week," adding: "The coat worn by the Captain of the pirate gang, the hatchet with which they were dispatched, and the secession flag which they manufactured out of the Union flag found on board of the schooner, will also be exhibited, and the particulars of the recapture of the schooner will be rehearsed to all who desire to hear them."[54]

On the same day that the *Times* story ran, the *Brooklyn Daily Eagle* revealed that Barnum had engaged Tillman and Stedding to appear in his museum, writing: "New York has got another hero, and Barnum (P. T. Barnum) has him on exhibition for the delight of all who patronize his singular establishment."[55] A notice in the *New York Herald* advertised that "WM. TILLMAN, THE COLORED STEWARD of the schooner S. J. Waring, WHO KILLED THE THREE PIRATES, and brought the vessel safely to the port with WILLIAM STEDDING, THE GERMAN SAILOR, will receive visitors at the Museum at all hours, and relate his experience with the Southern chivalry and exhibit the Secession Flag which the rebels made out of the American Flag; also a Rebel Cutlass, and THE IDENTICAL HATCHET WITH WHICH Tillman killed the ocean robbers."[56]

Frank Leslie's Weekly reported on July 27 that "the irrepressible Barnum, with his usual attention to the curiosity of the public, has engaged the 'heroic Nigger' [*sic*] who recaptured the *S. J. Waring* by killing the three pirates in possession. The German who was with him is also engaged."[57] And on August 10 *Frank Leslie's Illustrated Newspaper* reported that Barnum's museum was "abounding with novelties and amusements, as WM. TILLMAN and WM. STEDDING, the Conquerors of Southern Pirates, the Wonderful What Is It? Or Man Monkey, Madagascar Albinos, Aquarial Garden abounding with Living Fish, Diving sea lions, Mammoth Bear Samson and other Living Bears, Living Seals, and elegant Dramatic Performances every afternoon and evening. Admission to all, 25 cts. Children under ten years, 15 cts."[58]

An advertisement that appeared in the *Herald* on July 28 advised readers that excitement was "ON THE INCREASE" and that the public was "WILD WITH ENTHUSIASM" to see William Tillman. Tillman and Stedding, the advertisement said, were then "HOLDING DAILY LEVEES at the Museum, where they are entertaining visitors with interesting incidents of their eventful history."[59]

There is no evidence telling us whether Barnum paid Tillman and Stedding for their appearances at the museum, or if he did what the amount might have been. It seems more likely than not that he did, although it was probably not a large sum.

We do know, however, that Barnum made frequent use of

the popular lithography firm of Currier & Ives to advertise his presentations. Based at 152 Nassau Street, not far from Barnum's museum, Currier & Ives made a succession of at least thirty-five prints of notable Barnum featured acts, including one of Tillman. Produced to promote his appearance at the museum, their Tillman lithograph showed him in a stylish suit, complete with a vest, a white shirt and tie, and a comfortable coat. Two of the fingers of his right hand were inserted in the vest and his left hand rested jauntily on his hip. Tillman's suit was clearly a new one, probably presented to him by Barnum, although Tillman had at one time speculated that Jonas Smith would give him "a new suit of clothes" to reward him for saving the *Waring*.[60] The caption of the lithograph announced that he was "THE COLORED STEWARD, of the Schooner S. J. WARING, which was captured by the Piratical Brig JEFF DAVIS and recaptured by TILLMAN and WM. STEDDING the German Sailor after having killed three of the Pirates in charge of her. He is receiving Visitors daily at BARNUM'S MUSEUM, NEW YORK." The Currier & Ives lithograph would be the best image of Tillman to survive into our day.[61]

Tillman and Stedding's appearances at Barnum's museum ended on August 10, seventeen days after they began.[62] There is little doubt that Barnum had made money from them, although we can only guess at the amount, and that must have pleased him. But their appearances may also have reinforced his opposition to American slavery, for just four years later he loudly declared his candidacy for a seat in the Connecticut legislature for the specific purpose of voting in favor of the Thirteenth Amendment to the U.S. Constitution, ending slavery throughout the land. (Connecticut was Barnum's birthplace and the location of his country home, and the state's approval of the amendment would help to assure its ratification.) And after he won his legislative seat, he delivered a long and very eloquent address in favor of the amendment and racial equality. "Certainly, in the light of the great American spirit of liberty and equal rights which is sweeping over this country," Barnum then said, "and making the thrones of tyrants totter in the Old World, no party can afford to carry slavery, either of body or of mind. Knock off your manacles and let the man go free."[63]

Audience reactions to Tillman's appearances in Barnum's museum varied. Barnum had for years asked audiences to come to his museum to judge for themselves whether the acts and exhibits there were as advertised. If some spectators believed that Tillman was a hero and others regarded him as a villain or cutthroat—even a murderer; if some thought the Confederate privateers he had attacked with his hatchet and tossed into the sea were honorable combatants in a legitimate war while others regarded them as pirates deserving of the legal penalty of hanging, Barnum would have been satisfied, and happy to pocket the money Tillman brought into his coffers.[64]

But the ultimate assessment of Tillman's acts would not be made by Barnum or his audiences, but by others and in a different venue. And it was into that venue that the black man's destiny was now to take him.

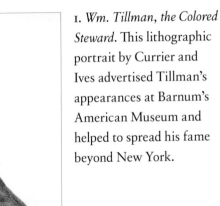

1. *Wm. Tillman, the Colored Steward.* This lithographic portrait by Currier and Ives advertised Tillman's appearances at Barnum's American Museum and helped to spread his fame beyond New York.

2. Merchant schooners like the *S. J. Waring* sailed the seas with valuable commercial cargos in the years leading up to and including the Civil War.

3. Jonas Smith, wealthy Long Island–based shipowner, employed William Tillman as cook and steward on his schooner *S. J. Waring*.

4. On April 17, 1861, Confederate president Jefferson Davis invited Southern privateers to go to sea to attack Union-based commercial vessels.

5. On April 19, 1861, Abraham Lincoln ordered a blockade of the Confederate coast and designated privateers as pirates.

6. On July 21, 1861, William Tillman brought the *S. J. Waring* back from its capture by Confederate privateers. The schooner is shown here lying safely at anchor in New York. Wood engraving from *Harper's Weekly*, August 3, 1861.

7. Cabin of the *S. J. Waring*. Wood engraving from *Harper's Weekly*, August 3, 1861.

8. William Tillman, the colored steward of the schooner *S. J. Waring*, killing the three pirates on board. Wood engraving from *Frank Leslie's Illustrated Newspaper*, August 3, 1861.

9. The attack on the second mate. Wood engraving from *Harper's Weekly*, August 3, 1861.

THE

AMERICAN COAST PILOT;

CONTAINING

DIRECTIONS

FOR THE

PRINCIPAL HARBORS, CAPES AND HEADLANDS

ON THE

COASTS OF NORTH AND SOUTH AMERICA;

DESCRIBING THE

SOUNDINGS, BEARINGS OF THE LIGHTHOUSES AND BEACONS FROM
THE ROCKS, SHOALS, LEDGES, &c.

WITH THE PREVAILING

WINDS, SETTING OF THE CURRENTS, &c.

AND THE

LATITUDES AND LONGITUDES

OF THE

PRINCIPAL HARBORS AND CAPES;

TOGETHER WITH

A TIDE TABLE.

BY EDMUND M. BLUNT.

EIGHTEENTH EDITION,
BY E. & G. W. BLUNT.

NEW-YORK:
PUBLISHED BY EDMUND AND GEORGE W. BLUNT,
179 WATER STREET, CORNER OF BURLING SLIP.
SEPTEMBER, 1857.

10. Title page of *Blunt's Coast Pilot*, the navigational guide the Irish passenger Bryce MacKinnon read from on the treacherous voyage back to New York.

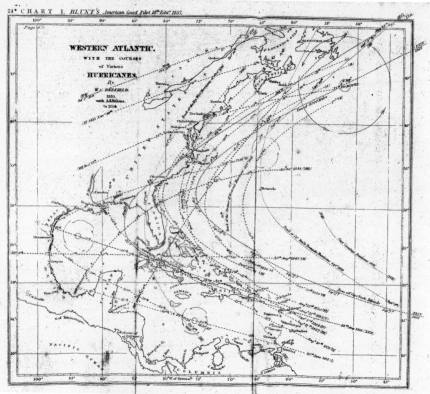

11. "Western Atlantic, with the Courses of Various Hurricanes," foldout chart from *Blunt's Coast Pilot.*

12. Portrait of William Tillman from the *American Phrenological Journal*, September 1861.

13. P. T. Barnum, legendary showman who invited William Tillman to appear in his American Museum.

14. Barnum's American Museum on lower Broadway, where William Tillman met curious visitors for seventeen days. Wood engraving from *Gleason's Pictorial Drawing-Room Companion.*

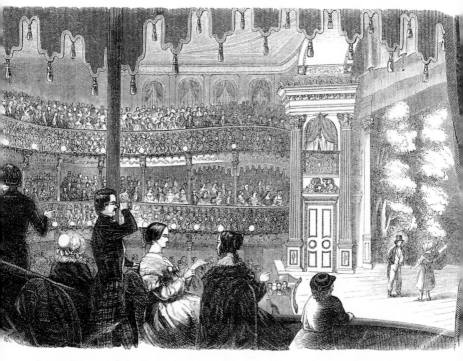

15. Interior view of the lecture room of the American Museum. Wood engraving from *Gleason's Pictorial Drawing-Room Companion*.

SEVEN

A MATTER OF COMPENSATION

Tillman's recapture of the *Waring* had legal and economic as well as military, political, and of course human implications. The schooner was a valuable vessel that had been seized at sea by Confederate privateers who sought to take it into a Southern port, where it and its even more valuable cargo would be sold and its owners would lose everything they had invested. Tillman and Stedding had risked their lives in a successful effort to bring the schooner back to New York, and in the process saved the owners from enormous losses. Under the law of salvage—an important part of both English and American law with roots extending as far back as Greek and Roman times—those who saved vessels and their cargoes from losses at sea were entitled to be rewarded for doing so. If Tillman and Stedding were in fact heroes and not villains, shouldn't they receive some monetary compensation for their heroism?

It is unlikely that either man realized at the outset that their recapture of the *Waring* might warrant any special compensation. There were, however, attorneys in New York who were quick to advise them of their rights, and eager to help enforce them. Certainly the insurance companies that had issued policies to cover losses suffered by the owners of the vessel and cargo knew that claims for salvage compensation were likely and that, if successful, they would be obligated to pay them. Knowing this, they were armed from the outset with the legal talent necessary to avoid doing so.

As New York in 1861 was the busiest and most profitable shipping center in the United States,[1] it was also the home to many admiralty lawyers, practitioners of an important branch of Anglo-American law that concerns itself with ships, cargoes, and associated property on the oceans and in navigable rivers and lakes.[2] The U.S. Constitution provides that the judicial power of the United States extends "to all cases of admiralty and maritime jurisdiction."[3] In 1789, the first Congress under the Constitution gave the federal district courts jurisdiction over admiralty cases and provided that they would be decided (as they had been in England) by judges sitting without juries.[4]

In New York the court with jurisdiction to hear salvage claims was the U.S. District Court for the Southern District of New York. It was presided over by Judge Samuel R. Betts with the assistance of Judge William Davis Shipman. Both judges were natives of Connecticut, but the seventy-five-year-old Betts was a veteran of many years of judicial service while the forty-three-year-old Shipman was a relatively new arrival on the federal bench. Betts had been appointed to the U.S. District Court in New York by President John Quincy Adams in 1826 and had held his position continuously ever since. Shipman had been appointed judge of the U.S. District Court in Connecticut by President James Buchanan in March 1860. Although he still held his Connecticut post, Shipman had been temporarily assigned to New York to help with the onslaught of cases brought there by the war.[5]

The word "salvage" refers to compensation for services rendered in saving property or rescuing it from perils encountered at sea. A person who renders such services is deemed a "salvor."[6] The perils giving rise to salvage may arise from dangers lurking in the water—rocks, reefs, shoals, destructive waves, or the like—or in the air—winds, rains, sleet, snow, thunderstorms, lightning, even hurricanes. They may also arise from human activity—collisions between two or more vessels, deliberate sabotage, or the predations of pirates. The purpose of awarding salvage is to induce those who are in a position to aid imperiled vessels to make the necessary efforts to do so, with the amount of the compensation determined by the judge according to standards of fairness and equity.[7]

Elaborate rules of law were developed over the centuries by the admiralty courts to determine what was required by fairness and equity. In the middle of the nineteenth century, these rules were described and analyzed in a book written by William Marvin, judge of the U.S. District Court in Key West, Florida. So many ships were wrecked while passing through the treacherous straits separating Florida, Cuba, and the Bahamas that Marvin's court in Key West (in Union hands throughout the Civil War) was called on to adjudicate more salvage cases than any other in the country. Published in Boston in 1858, Marvin's *Treatise on the Law of Wreck and Salvage* discussed an important body of law that judges in other parts of the country needed to apply in deciding the salvage cases brought before them.[8]

Only one day after their return to New York, the *New York Times* reported that Tillman and Stedding had "discovered" that their recapture of the *Waring* entitled them to salvage.[9] They had no doubt been counseled by lawyers who practiced admiralty law. If the lawyers did not approach them directly, they were most likely put in touch by the district attorney, E. Delafield Smith. The *Times* reported that Donald McLeod, who had refused to help Tillman and Stedding recapture the *Waring*, was now anxious to pursue salvage compensation alongside the other men. Bryce MacKinnon had also decided that he should be regarded as a salvor. According to the *Times*, MacKinnon claimed that he was "entitled to an equal portion of the salvage, having assisted to put one of the privateers-men in irons, and afterwards helped to navigate the vessel into port." Sensing that the claims made by the different men might conflict, the *Times* observed that "some more questions of law are likely to arise out of this question of salvage."[10]

On Saturday, July 27, an opening pleading in an action for salvage (formally called a "libel") was filed in Judge Betts's court by Charles E. Whitehead and William Curtis Noyes in behalf of William Tillman, William Stedding, and Donald McLeod.[11] Whitehead and Noyes were prominent New York attorneys with abundant experience in the practice of admiralty law. Following the usual principles of that law, they filed their libel against the *S. J. Waring* and its cargo but not against the owners. If salvage was awarded, it would become a lien against the schooner and its cargo and not a personal judgment against the owners, but if the owners (or their insurers) did not pay it, the schooner and its cargo would be sold at public action to satisfy the lien. Of course the insurers understood that if an award was made against the *Waring* and its cargo they would either have to pay it or work out some other arrangement (by way of settlement) that would satisfy the parties and their attorneys. The libel was sworn to by Tillman, Stedding, and McLeod before notaries public. Their signatures were affixed, however, not by writing their names but by each making a large letter X in the place indicated by the notaries.[12]

The libel began by reciting the facts necessary to give Judge Betts's court jurisdiction. It alleged that Tillman was a seaman and steward of Providence, Rhode Island, that Stedding was a seaman of New York City, and that McLeod was a seaman of Cape Breton, Nova Scotia. The schooner *S. J. Waring* was a domestic vessel built and owned in the United States by Jonas Smith & Co. The libel set out the basic facts of the case: The *Waring* had set sail from New York for Buenos Aires on July 4; it had been captured on July 7 by an armed brig calling itself the *Jeff Davis*, whose officers and men came aboard the schooner, claimed it as a prize of war, and installed a prize crew; the brig belonged to and sailed "in the name of a rebel faction calling itself the Confederate States of America" and carried what was claimed to be a letter of marque "issued by the said rebel faction." The libel recalled the nine days of voyage that followed the capture—a voyage toward an unnamed Southern port in which the schooner would be condemned and sold at public auction. Then, on July 16, when the *Waring* was only fifty miles south and one hundred miles east of Charleston, South Carolina, Tillman and Stedding managed to recapture the schooner. The libel said that their actions were motivated "by the love of liberty by which they were endowed by their Creator as well as by a laudable desire to rescue property in the hands of pirates." With his own hand, Tillman "slew the master and the two mates of the said prize crew with the hatchet which he had previously concealed," and Stedding helped him "cast their bodies into the sea." Tillman put the two remaining Confederates in chains and "assumed the command of the schooner." Though he possessed "little knowledge of navigation" and was "without the ordinary instruments of observation or possessing the knowledge to employ them," he was able to set the vessel back on course to New York. Exercising "great care, vigilance and forethought," he, Stedding, and McLeod were able to prevent the seizure of the schooner by the two Confederates who remained aboard, or "by any vessel sailing under a commission from the so-called Confederate States of America." Thus they brought the *Waring* to New York, where it arrived "in perfect safety on Sunday the 21st day of July." By their actions the ship and cargo "were saved to the owners and all others concerned, having received no other damage than the ordinary wear and tear such a voyage would justify." The libel alleged that the *Waring* was worth twelve thousand dollars at the time of its capture and that its cargo was worth seventy thousand dollars. "Wherefore and by reason of said bold and hazardous services your libellants are entitled to a proper salvage and said claim for salvage is a lien upon said vessel and cargo."[13]

On August 2 an admiralty attorney named James Thomson filed another libel in Betts's court, this seeking salvage for Bryce MacKinnon. MacKinnon offered a statement of what happened aboard the *Waring* on its fateful voyage that corresponded closely to the one made by Tillman, Stedding, and McLeod. He recounted the recapture of the schooner by Tillman and Stedding (a recapture he said subjected him to "great risk") and then described the assistance he had given Tillman and Stedding in bringing the vessel back to New York. He recalled that he gave them a pistol and some ammunition he owned so they could resist any attempt by the two remaining Confederates to retake the vessel. He helped to work the schooner as it moved northward. Recognizing that Tillman, Stedding, and McLeod were "entirely destitute of education and unable to read and write," he consulted *Blunt's Coast Pilot* for help in directing the vessel toward its destination. He took soundings of the ocean depth and directed the other men's attention to relevant passages in the *Coast Pilot* "without which the said vessel might probably have been lost." MacKinnon thought the *Waring* was worth twelve thousand dollars when it was captured by the privateers, though his estimate of the value of the cargo was lower than that of Tillman, Stedding, and McLeod: He set it at fifty thousand dollars. Following the example of the other men, MacKinnon alleged that the "care

and diligence" he had shown in rendering "hazardous services" aboard the schooner entitled him to "a proper salvage,"
which constituted a lien on the vessel and cargo.[14]

In accordance with the established procedure of salvage
courts, Judge Betts consolidated the two libels for trial.[15]
Also following established procedure, U.S. Marshal Murray
attached and seized the *Waring* and its cargo as security for
the payment of any salvage awards the court might make, and
Jonas Smith and the owners of the cargo filed papers establishing their ownership and posting bonds as security for payment
of the awards.[16] Thus it was possible to release the schooner
from attachment quickly and permit Smith to ready it for a
second attempt to complete its voyage to South America. The
owners of the cargo wanted their property to be delivered
to the persons who had contracted to purchase it, and Jonas
Smith wanted to put his schooner back into profitable service
as quickly as possible. War or no war, hatchet slayings or no
hatchet slayings, there was money to be made in shipping out
of the port of New York, and those who knew how to make it
did not want legal wrangling to interfere with their business.

Yet another attorney made an appearance in the case on
August 23. He was Townsend Scudder, a prominent admiralty
practitioner with offices in Manhattan and deep family roots
on Long Island.[17] Acting in behalf of Jonas Smith, whose own
Long Island roots may have provided some tie to Scudder, and
some twenty-six named cargo owners, Scudder filed a lengthy
answer to the libels of Tillman, Stedding, McLeod, and Mac-

Kinnon. It admitted that Tillman, Stedding, and McLeod were seamen aboard the *Waring* when it left New York, and that MacKinnon was a passenger, but it stated that neither Smith (who was identified as the sole owner of the schooner) nor the cargo owners had any personal knowledge of what had happened after the vessel left New York bound for South America. The answer claimed that the schooner and cargo were both worth less than the libels had stated: The *Waring* itself was valued at only nine thousand dollars and the cargo at thirty thousand. (Lower values would of course tend to reduce the amount of any salvage that might be awarded in the case.) Scudder argued that MacKinnon "did nothing toward the rescue" of the *Waring*, and that since Tillman, Stedding, and McLeod were in the employ of Jonas Smith the whole time the ship was at sea, they were "in duty bound by the law of the land to stand by and defend and protect said vessel and cargo." In their rescue of the schooner, the answer continued, they "did no more than under the circumstances they were hired and in duty bound to do." They were thus entitled to no salvage.[18]

These arguments were not completely unexpected. Judge Marvin's *Treatise on the Law of Wreck and Salvage* stated that whether a person employed aboard a ship at sea could ever be entitled to salvage for saving the ship was "a question upon which great judges have differed." The interests of the seamen were bound up with the safety of the ships they were employed on, Marvin said, so they were under a legal duty to try to save them from perils or attacks. If a ship was wrecked, for example, the ship's crewmen were "bound by the nature of their engagements, in their character of seamen, to obey the master's orders, and to remain by the ship or wreck, afloat or ashore, as long as there is a reasonable hope of saving anything without too much hazard of life." Seamen who discharged their preexisting legal duties were not entitled to salvage for doing so; they were entitled only to their wages. Marvin made it clear, however, that there were important exceptions to this general rule, and that there were circumstances that freed the seamen from their ordinary duties aboard an imperiled ship, and entitled them to salvage if they came to its rescue.[19]

A somewhat more surprising argument was now introduced. Scudder acknowledged the peculiar danger that Tillman faced while he was under the control of the Confederate privateers. He admitted that they had repeatedly spoken about his value as a slave and "threatened as soon as they arrived in the port of Charleston, to which they were bound, to sell him into slavery." Once he arrived in the Confederate states, Tillman was in fact liable to be sold into slavery, and Stedding, who was "an able-bodied man [and] in every respect suitable for a soldier," was in danger of being conscripted into the Confederate military. But whatever Tillman and Stedding did to recapture the *Waring* from the privateers they also did to rescue themselves from dangers to which they were personally subject—and not to save Jonas Smith's schooner or the cargo it carried. Tillman's object was to save himself from slavery, and Stedding's to avoid becoming a Confederate soldier. For these reasons Scudder's answer (personally signed under oath by Jonas Smith) forcefully declared that Tillman and Stedding were "not entitled to salvage."[20]

Preparations were now under way to try the issues raised by Tillman's, Stedding's, McLeod's, and MacKinnon's libels, and the sharply conflicting answers filed in behalf of Smith and the cargo owners. The trial promised to be a spirited, perhaps even a bitter, contest and—because it was part of a significant chapter in the awful war now spreading through the United States—an important one as well. But it was not the only legal battle raised by the secession of the Confederate states, or the only one that would find its way into courts of law.

Abraham Lincoln had condemned the Confederate effort to sever its ties with the United States as rebellion while Jefferson Davis and his supporters had defended it as a legitimate assertion of national independence. The conflict that was now growing in ferocity was, the Confederates argued, no rebellion but a legitimate war—a contest between two competing sovereigns comparable to the many disputes fought out on the high seas and in continental Europe between France and Britain, or France and Prussia, or Austria and the Ottoman Empire. The decision of the British government, embodied in a proclamation made by Queen Victoria on May 13, to recognize the Confederacy as a belligerent (a state actually at war) and to declare British neutrality between the United States and the Confederate states, strengthened the Confederate argument. The conflict was, the British insisted, an international war.[21]

But Queen Victoria's proclamation did not settle the troubling issue that still divided the North and the South. History would soon reveal that a resolution of the issue would have to be sought on the battlefields where troops in blue and gray would meet each other in mortal combat. In the meantime, however, the courts would be called on to address the same issue, and to provide at least a tentative answer to it. And to men like William Tillman, even the tentative answer would be important, for it would powerfully affect their lives.

EIGHT

PASSING JUDGMENT

The *Waring* was not the only merchant ship that found itself embroiled in the dispute raging between Washington, D.C., and Richmond, Virginia. Other vessels, many still powered by sail but more and more propelled by new and powerful steam engines, were attempting to continue their voyages across the Atlantic, southward into the Caribbean, or along the coast of South America, hoping to avoid potentially catastrophic contact with the privateers and blockading vessels now prowling the seas.

Early in June the Confederate privateer *Savannah* had been hauled into New York, brought before the U.S. District Court there, and judicially condemned as a war prize.[1] There was no real question that the *Savannah* was a Confederate privateer and, as such, subject to confiscation in U.S. courts. The real issue revealed itself when thirteen members of the *Savannah*'s crew were brought into New York aboard a separate U.S. Navy ship and put on trial in the U.S. Circuit Court. The charge lodged against them was piracy.[2]

Piracy was a serious criminal offense—proscribed by congressional enactments dating as far back as 1790, and punishable by death.[3] But were the Southerners who sailed aboard the *Savannah* and successfully captured two Northern merchant ships before their raids were halted by Yankee intervention really pirates? Were they common robbers who prowled the oceans preying on private ships? Or were they the duly authorized representatives of a sovereign nation—the Confederate States of America—and, as such, warriors in a legitimate struggle for national independence? These were the questions the jury assembled in the circuit court in New York was called on to decide in a trial that began on Wednesday, October 23, 1861.

Under the circuit-riding system that then prevailed in the federal courts, the circuit court was presided over by two judges: Samuel Nelson, a New York–based associate justice of the U.S. Supreme Court, and William Davis Shipman of Connecticut, still on temporary assignment as a district judge in New York.[4]

One day before the trial of the *Savannah* crew began in New York, a similar trial opened in the U.S. Circuit Court in Philadelphia, where William Wallace Smith, a former harbor pilot from Savannah, Georgia, was also charged with the capital crime of piracy. Smith had been one of the original privateers aboard the *Jeff Davis* when it left Charleston on June 28.[5] On July 6, the day before the *Davis* captured the *Waring*, it seized the Yankee schooner *Enchantress* off Nantucket and installed Smith as prize captain. Smith promptly turned the *Enchantress* south toward Charleston, where it would be condemned and sold as a war prize. Left aboard the captured schooner,

however, was a twenty-five-year-old steward and cook named
Jacob Garrick. Born in the Danish West Indies,* Garrick, like
Tillman, was a free black man with an aversion to being sold
into slavery. When he heard Smith say that he would "fetch
fifteen hundred dollars when we get him into Charleston," he
was understandably distressed.[6] Only two weeks later, however, a U.S. gunboat named the *Albatross* encountered the
Enchantress off Cape Hatteras and approached it to inquire
about its status. Anxious to conceal their identity as privateers,
Smith and his crew ran up the Stars and Stripes and loudly
protested that they were loyal Yankees. But Garrick put the
lie to their protests. He leaped over the rail of the *Enchantress*,
swam toward the *Albatross*, and shouted for all to hear that the
Enchantress was in fact a captured vessel of the privateer *Jeff
Davis* and "they are taking her into Charleston."[7] Garrick's
shouts alerted the Yankees to the deception. They hauled the
black man up onto the *Albatross*, boarded the *Enchantress*,
and quickly confirmed that it was under Confederate control.
Then they put the prize crew into irons and headed for Philadelphia. When they arrived there, Smith was arrested and
charged with piracy. The U.S. Circuit Court in Philadelphia
was then presided over by Robert Grier, a Pennsylvania-based
associate justice of the United States Supreme Court, and
John Cadwalader, the U.S. district judge in Philadelphia. Grier
and Cadwalader were both on the bench, facing the witnesses,

---

*Since 1917, the United States Virgin Islands of St. Thomas, St. John, and
St. Croix.

the lawyers, and the jury, when the trial of William Wallace Smith began on October 22.[8]

The evidence that the juries heard in the trials in New York and Philadelphia did not conflict much. The defendants in both cases were unquestionably Confederate privateers. They had prowled the seas in search of Northern shipping vessels and, when they found them, used threats of force to seize them and take them to Southern ports to be condemned and sold; or, if that was impractical, burn them at sea. They had been authorized to do just this by letters of marque issued by the government of President Jefferson Davis.[9] They had agreed among themselves that they would divide the spoils of their privateering, each taking a share of the proceeds of sale of the captured vessels, so that each would profit in some way from the captures. Their defense was not that they were not privateers. It was that, because they were *privateers*, they were not *pirates*. If they had to be detained, it was as prisoners of war, not as criminals. If they were to be punished, they argued, it was by being held in Yankee prisons and not dangled from ropes hung from Yankee gallows.

Long arguments were made by defense attorneys in both New York and Philadelphia likening the Confederates to the patriots who had fought for independence from Britain in the American Revolution. Not everybody in 1776 agreed that George Washington, John Adams, Alexander Hamilton, and Thomas Jefferson were freedom fighters; many—American "Tories" among them—believed that they were rebels, traitors to the British Crown, and thus no better than criminals who deserved to be hanged. But they were eventually recognized as combatants in a war and acclaimed as patriotic heroes. It was not necessary to agree with the propriety of the Confederate secession to admit that it had happened. Acts of the Continental Congress during the Revolution were the political equivalents of acts of the government of the Confederate states. The war that now raged between the North and the South may not have been a war in the eyes of the law, but it was a war in fact and had to be recognized as such by the jurors in New York and Philadelphia.[10]

The piracy case went to the jury in Philadelphia on October 25. Judge Grier was the first of the two judges to deliver instructions to the jury. He was a Democrat who had been appointed to the Supreme Court in 1846 by President James K. Polk, a Democrat and slaveholder from Tennessee, and he had never shown any judicial hostility to the slaveholding South. (He was in fact one of the judges who concurred in the result of Chief Justice Roger Taney's searingly controversial opinion in the *Dred Scott* case in 1857, although he expressed his own reasons for doing so.)[11] In the present case, however, Grier's opinions were not friendly to the Confederacy. He reviewed the evidence in the case and the arguments made by the defense attorneys but largely rejected them. He said he could view the Southern rebels "in no other light than [as] traitors to their country, and those who assume by their authority a right to plunder the property of our citizens on the high seas as pirates." Grier thought that the Confederate states had descended into "national insanity."[12] They had seceded from the Union not because they were oppressed, but because they disagreed with the outcome of the 1860 election. "Why prate about the right of an oppressed people to change their government by a revolution?" he asked. "Can that justify the treason and rebellion of those who were never oppressed, but who seek to substitute a military tyranny for the purpose of conquest and oppression?"[13] Following Grier, Judge Cadwalader's instructions addressed some technical points raised during the trial but did not disagree in substance with his colleague's views.[14]

The New York piracy case went to the jury on October 30. There Nelson was the only judge who addressed the jury. Like Grier, Nelson was a Democrat who had concurred in Taney's famous (some said infamous) *Dred Scott* decision, though his pro-Southern sympathies may have been even stronger than Grier's.[15] Nelson had been appointed to the Supreme Court in 1845 by the slaveholding (and later pro-secessionist) President John Tyler of Virginia. He revealed a lot more sympathy for the defense arguments than Grier. He expressed doubts whether anyone authorized by a government could be deemed a "pirate" when he was authorized only to attack the ships of one nation. Pirates were by definition freelance robbers who could attack and capture the ships of any nation or people, but Confederate privateers were authorized only to seize ships belonging to the states of the Union. Nelson noted the elaborate arguments made by the defense comparing the Confederate secession to the American Revolution—arguments that Grier roundly rejected—but he declined to consider them. He thought they raised political and not legal questions, and that those questions should be addressed by the executive and legislative branches of the government, not by the courts. He did not reject them outright, however. The jury had heard defense lawyers expound at great length on these arguments, and Nelson made no special efforts to rebut them.

The jury in New York deliberated for some twenty hours before returning to the courtroom and informing Judges Nelson and Shipman that they could not agree. The final vote was eight to four for the prosecution, but that was not enough for conviction, so the jury was dismissed.[16] The jury in Philadelphia deliberated for only forty-five minutes before returning with a unanimous verdict. The defendant there was guilty of the crime of piracy and would be sentenced to death for his offense.[17]

Other privateers were brought into New York and Philadelphia, but they were not executed—they were not even put on trial—for political events more powerful even than the United States statutes condemning piracy intervened. As soon as Jefferson Davis heard that men holding his letters of marque were being charged with the crime of piracy, he wrote Lincoln warning him not to execute any of them. He argued that they should be treated as prisoners of war in the same way as soldiers captured on a battlefield. As such, they should be exchanged for Northern prisoners held by the Confederacy or, if not exchanged, held in confinement until they could ultimately be exchanged. If any Confederates were executed, Davis threatened to retaliate by executing Northern prisoners of like rank.[18]

The Lincoln administration now reconsidered its policy and decided not to proceed with any more criminal trials. The accused pirates were not sentenced. They were transferred to military prisons and ultimately exchanged for Northern prisoners held by the Confederacy.[19] Davis's argument obviously had some force. Beyond that, however, Lincoln and his advisers considered it more important that the legal point be made—that Confederate privateers were criminal pirates in the eyes of the law—than that their blood be shed to prove the point.[20]

The jury in the New York trial of the *Savannah* privateers had not yet concluded its deliberations when Judge Shipman opened the salvage trial of *Tillman et al. v. The Schooner S. J. Waring*, on Monday, October 28, in the same court. The U.S. courts were then crowded with important cases, some brought on by the war, others relating more exclusively to continuing business operations in New York, so the district judge's absence from the *Savannah* case was not surprising. When the jury returned to court, Judge Nelson could answer any questions they might ask him, and decide if and when the jury should be dismissed for its failure to agree on a verdict.

Somewhat surprisingly only four witnesses were called to testify in the salvage case, and all four were men who were seeking to receive salvage awards. Tillman was the first, followed by Stedding, MacKinnon, and then McLeod. The black steward and cook was examined at length, and the answers he gave to the lawyers' questions fully bore out the statements he had made before the trial to newspaper reporters, the U.S. marshal, and the U.S. district attorney. He was not at all shy about relating the facts of his attack on the three prize officers aboard the schooner. He made it clear that when he learned of the Confederates' intentions to take him to a Southern port and sell him into slavery, he firmly decided that he would not suffer that fate. After he recaptured the *Waring*, he worked the vessel northward, attempting to avoid dangers both in the sea and on the shore. He acknowledged the help he received from Stedding, although he minimized MacKinnon's contributions to the successful voyage north. "MacKinnon never gave me any directions," Tillman said. "He knew nothing about trimming sails or changing the course. He did not put his hand to the wheel from the time we took the vessel until we got to New York. All MacKinnon did was to keep watch with Stedding." He admitted that MacKinnon had consulted *Blunt's Coast Pilot* to identify particular locations along the coast, but he did not think the information he retrieved was of much help, for they had already passed most of the locations MacKinnon read about. He admitted that McLeod, who had initially refused to help him recapture the *Waring*, did his part in helping to bring the schooner back to New York, where it finally arrived on July 21.[21]

Stedding's testimony agreed in every important fact with what Tillman had said about the voyage back to New York. He informed Judge Shipman that he was born in Germany, that he had followed the sea for five years, and that Jonas Smith had hired him to join the crew of the *Waring* only one day before it departed for South America. "I can't read or write English," Stedding admitted, "or take an observation. I never studied navigation."[22]

Bryce MacKinnon's testimony was more extensive than Stedding's. He told the judge that he was twenty-three years old and had been born in County Antrim, Ireland. He had lived in the United States for almost four years, most of that time in Manhattan. He had booked passage on the *Waring* for Montevideo, Uruguay, because of arrangements he had made with friends to purchase some land there and possibly go into stock breeding. He testified at some length about Tillman's hatchet attacks on the prize officers: He was in his cabin berth at night when he heard Montague Amiel, the prize captain, "give a kind of scream." He rose and watched through the open door as Tillman struck the captain and then the second mate with his hatchet, then went up on deck to attack the first mate with the same weapon. It was an awful scene that sent "a thrill of terror" over the Irishman. But after that thrill passed, he said, "I knew everything—everything was clear." Asked how long the "thrill of terror" lasted, he said that it was "just like a touch of a battery . . . just as quick as the blood could pass through the body—I believe it was just as quick as that." When Tillman told him to "be still," he immediately complied. But almost as quickly he began to help Tillman, Stedding, and McLeod in their efforts to save the *Waring*. He gave them the pistol and ammunition he had brought aboard, and he helped them put the two remaining Confederates, Milnor and Dorsett, in irons. Asked by one of the attorneys if he had willingly helped Tillman, Stedding, and McLeod, MacKinnon answered that he had: "I was quite willing to assist them."[23]

MacKinnon testified at some length about the ordeal the men aboard the schooner went through as they struggled to navigate the *Waring* back toward New York, and about the efforts he had made to help them do so. He told Judge Shipman that it was his idea to consult *Blunt's Coast Pilot* and that, since he was the only man aboard the schooner who was able to read, it fell to him to study key passages from the book and read them to Tillman, Stedding, and McLeod.

Asked whether he knew when he was aboard the *Waring* that he "would be entitled to salvage" if the vessel made it back to New York, he said that the idea "did not come into my head." But he recalled conversing with Tillman about whether the black man would be entitled to some sort of reward for what he had done in saving the vessel from its Confederate captors. The conversation took place "when the steward was taking out the bloody clothes, to pitch them over." Tillman said then that he thought he would be allowed to sell the remainder of the clothes when he got to New York. "He also said he expected the owners to give him a new suit of clothes; he said he thought he was entitled to a new suit of clothes, and he believed the owner or owners would give him such. I said"—MacKinnon added dryly—"I thought he would get more than that." [24]

By the time the salvage trial had begun, the *Waring* had already left New York on its second attempt to sail to Montevideo and Buenos Aires. MacKinnon was asked why he didn't take passage on that voyage. Hadn't he received a letter from Jonas Smith informing him that the schooner was about to leave New York? (The suggestion here was that the Irishman preferred to remain in New York to collect salvage money rather than complete his voyage south.) Yes, MacKinnon admitted, he had received such a letter from Smith, but it didn't offer him free passage on the *Waring*. He understood that he could go, but he would be expected to pay a second fare to do so. He decided to stay in New York.[25]

McLeod's testimony was the shortest of all. He admitted that he had refused to help Tillman and Stedding recapture the *Waring* from the privateers. Asked if he had gotten "any information out of any books," he said he had not, explaining: "I can't read printing. I can't read writing. I can't write." [26]

No witnesses were called by the attorneys for Jonas Smith or the cargo owners. All the attorneys had agreed as to the values properly assignable to the schooner and each of the items of its cargo, so it was not necessary to present evidence on that point. And the attorneys for the owners apparently did not believe that the testimony given by the claimants was anything other than credible and convincing. The critical issue in the case was not what had happened aboard the *Waring* on its fateful voyage, but what the legal consequences of those events would be.

When the testimony concluded, Judge Shipman asked the attorneys to submit written statements of the legal principles and authorities (formally called "points and authorities") the judge should consider in deciding the case.[27] He then listened to oral arguments.

The owners' attorneys (backed up by their insurers) argued very forcefully that none of the men now claiming salvage for saving the *Waring* were entitled to receive it. Tillman was an employee of Jonas Smith & Co. and, as such, obligated by the terms of his employment to do all he could to save the schooner from the privateers. He received wages for his work on the vessel and was not entitled to any extra compensation for taking it back from the Confederates—doing that was simply a part of his job. The same argument applied to Stedding and McLeod.

Strong arguments—these overlaid with a tone of bitterness—were made about the character of Tillman and Stedding's actions in retaking the schooner. The attorneys for the owners condemned them for their "sanguinary character." They insisted that the two men, especially Tillman, "exhibited ferocity rather than valor" when they attacked the officers of the prize crew. They took human lives; they shed human blood, and they did so deliberately and brutally. They should not receive any salvage for killing the three men aboard the *Waring*; or, if they did receive any, it should be greatly reduced because of the deplorable way in which they did it.

The owners' attorneys also argued that Tillman and Stedding's claims for salvage should be denied because their recapture of the *Waring* was not beneficial to the schooner. By putting it under "the sole control of uneducated and unskillful navigators" it actually increased the schooner's peril. It would have been better to let it continue its voyage into Charleston. The attorneys argued that the United States had a legal duty to restore the property of loyal citizens that was taken by the Confederates, and that the courts ought to presume that this would in fact be done.

The final argument against Tillman's claim for salvage was that he had been motivated by a desire to escape "the doom of slavery" and not by any intention of saving the *Waring* or its cargo. Yes, he had good reason to fear that when he reached Charleston he would be put on the auction block. The privateers, who regarded black men as property and not as fellow-citizens, would sell him and divide the proceeds among them. It mattered not whether Tillman would bring a thousand dollars or fifteen hundred. Either amount would have been substantial enough to motivate the greed of the privateers and put Tillman in peril of losing his freedom.

Judge Shipman listened to all the arguments and then took the case under advisement. He was a busy judge and had to be ready when new cases were brought into his court. Confederate ships captured by blockading vessels were the source of some of these cases, though more of them probably resulted from the capture of foreign ships that were attempting to run Lincoln's blockade of the Confederate coast. The legal issues raised by these captures were complicated, as they dealt not only with American law but also with international obligations laid down in treaties and the well-established "law of nations." Shipman did not announce his decision in Tillman's case until late December.[28]

On Christmas Eve the judge's three-thousand-word opinion was printed in the *New York Times*. Most of the opinion was devoted to a recapitulation of the facts to which Tillman, Stedding, MacKinnon, and McLeod had testified. But a key part was used to announce that all four of the men who claimed salvage were entitled to receive it. Answering the argument that Tillman had acted in a "sanguinary" manner, Shipman conceded that "no Court ought to sanction or indirectly encourage unnecessary and wanton violence, even toward those who avow themselves the enemies of the nation." But in determining whether violence was necessary, "all the circumstances must be taken into consideration." The judge noted that the *Waring* had sailed from New York "on a peaceable and lawful voyage." He continued:

> She was overtaken on the high seas by an armed vessel—her officers and two of her crew taken from her, and made prisoners on board the capturing vessel—leaving but three of her crew and a passenger. McLeod refused to aid in the rescue—MacKinnon's views were unknown; Tillman and Stedding must alone encounter the three prize officers and the prize seamen, five in all. Their only arms were a small pocket-pistol, a knife and a hatchet. The peril of the undertaking was imminent and desperate. Instant death to both Stedding and Tillman would probably have followed their failure. They had a right to recapture the vessel if they could. They took the hazard, and, after having dispatched the three men they

had most to fear, they spared the other two, an equal
number with themselves. It is suggested that they ought
to have spared the officers, or some of them, after they
had wounded them. It is difficult to say what the precise
condition of the officers was after the first blows; but I
am inclined to think they were mortally wounded—and
it is not easy to see how Tillman and Stedding could have
extended to them any humane attentions. Their peril was
by no means at an end. They were near a hostile coast,
four or five days' sail from a place of safety, without the-
oretical knowledge of navigation, and by no means free
from danger of recapture by another armed cruiser. I
think they are not to be blamed for devoting their ener-
gies at once to their escape from peril by navigating their
vessel to a place of safety, instead of bestowing their
attentions upon their dying enemies.[29]

Shipman next addressed the argument that Tillman's rescue of the *Waring* did not relieve it from peril, but actually
increased it, because Tillman had no knowledge of navigation.
He said that he knew of "no principle of law that prescribes the
degree of knowledge a man must possess, as a condition prec-
edent to his performing salvage service when no other human
aid is within reach. Fidelity and success are of more account,
in the eye of the law, than accomplishments." He reviewed
some of the legal authorities on the point, including one cited
in Marvin's *Treatise on the Law of Wreck and Salvage* that said:
"Where persons offer their services to vessels in distress, and

there are no other individuals on the spot capable of rendering more efficient assistance, this Court must look with considerable indulgence at their efforts—because, being the only aid that can be procured, and offered in a state of great exigency, every allowance must be made if they are not possessed of adequate knowledge to perform the duty they had undertaken."[30] And another, also cited in Marvin, declared that "when persons undertake to perform a salvage service, they are bound to exercise ordinary skill and prudence in the execution of the duty they take upon themselves to perform." They need not be "finished navigators, but they must possess and exert such a degree of skill and prudence as persons in their condition ordinarily do possess, and may be fairly expected to display."[31] Shipman thought that "it would be a most extraordinary doctrine to hold, that when a vessel is found on the high seas, deprived of her officers and part of her crew, in the most certain and imminent peril of becoming lost to her owners, and she is by the faithful remnant of her crew rescued and brought safely into port, that her salvors, the only persons who could possibly have performed the service, are to be deprived of their reward because they were ignorant of the theory of navigation." He continued:

> It is sufficient in this case, that by the familiarity of Tillman, the colored steward, with the coast from the place of rescue to New-York; his accurate recollection and ready recognition of localities; his sleepless vigilance, and a courage and good sense that does him great credit,

he was able with the aid of his comrades to bring the vessel with so much speed and safety into port. Whether he was able to keep the log-book, or work out the dead reckoning cannot affect the value of the services rendered to the claimants.[32]

The judge referred briefly to the arguments of the owners' attorney that the court ought to presume that the United States would restore the *Waring* and its cargo to the owners and did not need to rely upon men like Tillman and Stedding to do so. Shipman dismissed this as "a purely speculative suggestion. . . . It is not for me, in disposing of present rights, to rest my conclusions upon what the Government will feel called upon to do, when the present furious strife shall have terminated. Courts of Admiralty, in administering public law, act upon facts and rules of law, and not upon speculations as to the course nations may pursue." [33]

Shipman devoted even less attention to the argument that, because Tillman was desperate to avoid "the doom of slavery," he was not entitled to any salvage for rescuing the *Waring*. "But it is settled law that the motives of the salvor are not to be inquired into," the judge wrote.[34]

The day after it published the full text of Judge Shipman's opinion, the *Times* expressed its approval of it. It noted in particular the arguments of the owners and their attorneys that Tillman's attack on the Confederates aboard the *Waring* was "an act marked with ferocity" and that the court should not countenance it. "But the Judge holds that in an attack by two men, armed only with a hatchet, a knife and a small pocket pistol, upon five men well-armed, the fact that three out of the five were killed is not one which diminishes the peril to the sailors, or the advantage to the owners of the vessel. We think public sentiment will sustain him in that conclusion. If the views of the claimants were correct, Tillman's act was murder, and he should have been tried and hung instead of rewarded."[35] In all, the *Times* felt that Shipman's decision "cannot fail to render the holding of captured vessels by prize crews much more difficult than it would otherwise be. Seamen will be more ready to incur the hazards of attempted recapture, and owners may well afford to reward them for incurring them."[36]

Shipman did not render a formal decree until February 6, 1862. In it he set the total amount of salvage to be awarded in the case at seventeen thousand dollars, with Tillman to receive seven thousand, Stedding six thousand, MacKinnon three thousand, and McLeod one thousand.[37] The attorneys for Jonas Smith and the cargo owners were apparently unsatisfied with this award, for they appealed the decree to the circuit court on April 8. Arguments were heard there before Judge Nelson on May 13, at which time the decree was quickly affirmed.

The court records are sketchy about what happened next. The decree was affirmed, but the records do not tell us if the full amount of the salvage award was actually paid. They state only that the case was "settled." This could mean that the insurance companies were still resistant to full payment, forcing Tillman and his fellow salvors to accept something less than the amounts the court ordered. Delay alone can be a bargaining chip in many court proceedings. Tillman's amount of Shipman's award was a very substantial sum of money in 1862, approaching the total value of the *S. J. Waring* itself. Although we do not know if he received it all, we know very clearly that Judge Shipman believed he should.

NINE

THE FURY CONTINUES

As the courts wrestled with the legal problems raised by the conflict between the North and the South, the fighting continued with awful fury.

Jefferson Davis had made it clear from the outset that his Confederate states sought independence so they could perpetuate and even expand the institution of chattel slavery in the South. Slavery had made cotton "king" in the Southern states and enabled the cotton-producing region to become one of the richest in the world. Davis not only believed that slaves were property—and thus protected by the Constitution—but also that slavery "was established by decree of Almighty God." He argued that slavery was "sanctioned in the Bible, in both Testaments, from Genesis to Revelations [*sic*]," that it had "existed in all ages," and that it "has been found among the people of the highest civilization, and in the nations of the highest proficiency in the arts."[1]

Addressing the Confederate Congress in April 1861, Davis accused Lincoln's Republican Party of advocating policies "rendering property in slaves so insecure as to be comparatively worthless," and declaring that the Confederate states were forced to adopt a "course of action to avert the danger with which they were openly menaced."[2] Speaking in Savannah in March 1861, Davis's vice president, Alexander Stephens, declared that the Confederate government was founded upon an implicit belief in African American slavery. "Its foundations are laid," Stephens said, "its corner-stone rests upon the great truth, that the negro is not equal to the white man; that slavery—subordination to the superior race—is his natural and normal condition."[3]

For his own part Lincoln hated the institution of slavery— he said he had always hated it—and believed that it should be put on the road to "ultimate extinction."[4] In one of his many reflective moments, he wrote: "As I would not be a slave, so I would not be a master. This expresses my idea of democracy. Whatever differs from this, to the extent of the difference, is no democracy."[5] But when he became president, Lincoln was cautious in his approach to the institution. He did not believe that the federal government had any power under the Constitution to interfere with slavery within any state.[6] Further, he was fearful that if he antagonized border states, where slavery was still legal, he would drive them into the arms of the Confederacy and thereby jeopardize the outcome of the war and the future of the Union.[7] If he kept the Union together, slavery would still remain on the road to "ultimate extinction." And so the war grew in size, intensity, and bitterness, with some at first denying that it had anything to do with African American slavery and others admitting that, yes, slavery was at the center of it and that that centrality would eventually have to be admitted.

African Americans themselves never had any serious doubts about what the war was about, or where their hopes for freedom lay. Literate or illiterate, educated or uneducated, living in cities and towns or on plantations in the most remote reaches of the South, they heard the news about secession, about the fall of Fort Sumter, and about the beginning of hostilities between the North and the South, and in their hearts and minds they, like William Tillman, cast their lot with the North.[8] If the grapevine was their principal source of news, it functioned dependably.[9] Word was sent from North to South and back again, keeping the slaves reliably informed.

Early in the war African Americans made efforts to join the Union army and navy. They volunteered to fight with militia units and requested permission to form all-black units that could fight alongside their white comrades. But their requests were almost always denied.[10] An act of Congress passed in 1792 had limited membership in the state militias to white men, and since the first Union forces were drawn largely from the militias, they were also limited to whites.[11] Beyond the law, however, most whites did not consider blacks capable of military service. They could provide noncombatant support for white troops—working as laborers, cooks, waiters, guards, blacksmiths, and teamsters—but they could not handle firearms responsibly or respond dependably to military discipline. As one New York corporal wrote to his sister, "We don't want to fight side and side with the nigger. We think we are a too superior race for that."[12] When blacks in Cincinnati offered to form a company of "Home Guards" to protect the city against possible Confederate attack, they were repulsed with the angry words of a white Cincinnatian: "This is a white man's war, and you d——d niggers must keep out of it."[13]

Of course blacks helped to support the Confederate armies in the South. They were slaves and had to obey the orders they were given. When entrenchments and fortifications had to be built, black slaves were commandeered from plantations to build them. When heavy guns had to be dragged from place to place, they were ordered to drag them. When stables had to be cleaned, slaves obeyed their orders and cleaned them. Most of the food that supported the Southern troops was grown by black laborers in the fields that stretched from Virginia south and west to Louisiana and Texas.[14] Some blacks—even some free blacks—in Southern states made special efforts to help the Confederates—they drove wagons and donated farm products to help feed hungry Confederate troops. But far more blacks volunteered to join the Union.

On August 6, 1861, only two weeks after William Tillman's return to New York aboard the *S. J. Waring*, Congress passed a "confiscation act" authorizing the Union seizure of all property, including slaves, used in aiding, abetting, or promoting the Southern "insurrection."[15] On April 16, 1862, it abolished slavery in the nation's capital, declaring that "all persons held to service or labor within the District of Columbia by reason of African descent" were immediately freed.[16] And on July

17, 1862, it passed a second "confiscation act," declaring that all slaves of rebel masters, including those who escaped into Union lines, would be "forever free," and authorizing the president "to employ as many persons of African descent" as he deemed necessary for the suppression of the rebellion.[17]

Lincoln signed all these laws, adding his encouragement to the hopes of African Americans that they would soon be recognized as free men and women throughout the country. But he did even more on September 22, 1862, when he announced his preliminary Emancipation Proclamation, and on January 1, 1863, when he issued his final instrument bearing the same name, a history-making document declaring that the slaves in all parts of the nation then in rebellion "are, and henceforward shall be free," and further proclaiming that they would be "received into the armed service of the United States to garrison forts, positions, stations, and other places, and to man vessels of all sorts in said service."[18] It was now clearer than ever before that the military fortunes of the North and the hopes of blacks to escape the last shackles of slavery were inextricably tied together.

But there was still some very bitter opposition to the abolition of slavery, and to the reception of black soldiers into the military. On March 3, 1863, Congress enacted a conscription law that required all "able-bodied male citizens" between the ages of twenty and forty-five to register for the draft and that made no distinctions as to race. Draftees could, however, avoid service by paying a three-hundred-dollar commutation fee.[19] As federal officials began to put the new law into effect, renewed resentment against African Americans was expressed in different parts of the country. White opponents of the freedom of slaves, and of their reception into the Union forces, argued that freed African Americans would promptly leave their Southern plantations for Northern cities and towns to take jobs away from poor whites. They would be nothing less than an invading force. The rising tide of anti-black sentiment found its most extreme expression in New York City where, on July 13, 1863, gangs of poor, mostly Irish immigrants embarked on a bloody rampage against the city's blacks. Screaming, "Kill all niggers!" they swarmed into African American neighborhoods, lynching blacks from trees and lampposts and attacking many in their homes. So unbridled was their anger they even burned the Colored Orphan Asylum to the ground. The New York City draft riots were soon recognized as the largest single incident of civil disorder in the history of the United States.[20] The carnage and violence continued for four days, and then abated. Hoping to avoid more riots, Lincoln sent new military reinforcements to the city, and committees of pro-Union New Yorkers offered relief to the suffering.

Almost immediately following the New York draft riots, in far-distant South Carolina, a unit of all-black soldiers began an assault on a Confederate fortification that guarded the entrance to Charleston Harbor. The unit was the Fifty-Fourth Massachusetts Volunteer Infantry Regiment, organized in early 1863 at the request of the Massachusetts governor, John Andrew, and with the approval of U.S. Secretary of War Edwin

Stanton. With white officers (blacks were not yet trusted to command fighting units), the Fifty-Fourth initially included a thousand African Americans drawn from all the Northern states, plus some from Canada.[21] The regiment was on the sea-coast of South Carolina on July 18, preparing a furious assault on Fort Wagner, a heavily armed earthen redoubt only a mile and a half from Fort Sumter. The black soldiers fought val-iantly through the night, eventually gaining the parapet of the fort and holding it for an hour before they were driven back. Nearly half the men in the regiment were killed, including its white commanding colonel, Robert Gould Shaw. Apprised of the assault on Fort Wagner, the Northern press praised the courage and valor of the black soldiers. A letter sent to the *New York Times* declared: "Could anyone from the North see these brave fellows as they lie here, their prejudice against them, if he had any, would all pass away."[22]

In December 1863, an all-black unit, the Twentieth Regi-ment United States Colored Troops, was formed in New York, and on March 5, 1864, it marched to a gigantic rally in Union Square. The *Times* applauded the event, writing that "eight months ago the African race in this City were literally hunted down like wild beasts. They fled for their lives. When caught, they were shot down in cold blood, or stoned to death, or hung to the trees or the lamp-posts." Now the same men "march in solid platoons, with shouldered muskets, slung knapsacks, and buckled cartridge-boxes down through our gayest ave-nues and our busiest thoroughfares to the pealing strains of martial music, and are everywhere saluted with waving handkerchiefs, with descending flowers, and with the acclamations and plaudits of countless beholders."[23]

Before the war came to an end, more than 180,000 African Americans fought in the Union army and upwards of 19,000 saw service in the navy. Most of the fighting between the North and the South ended on Palm Sunday, April 9, 1865, at Appomattox Court House in Virginia, when Confederate general Robert E. Lee surrendered his Confederate army to Union forces led by Lt. Gen. Ulysses S. Grant. At Appomattox witnessing the surrender were seven black regiments comprising two thousand black troops.[24] Slavery did not end until eight months later, when the Thirteenth Amendment to the U.S. Constitution was ratified, abolishing slavery throughout the land. Lincoln had been a strong supporter of the amendment and made strenuous efforts to get it through Congress. But he did not live to see its final ratification, which came on December 6, 1865. Many lives had been lost in the course of the war, and many heroes had been acclaimed. Abraham Lincoln himself was one of the more than six hundred thousand estimated casualties.

William Tillman, by the estimates of many, still ranked as—if not the very first—at least one of the first heroes of the war.

Some of the praise showered on Tillman still echoed through the land. Frederick Douglass's impassioned estimate of Tillman as "A Black Hero," first published in *Douglass' Monthly* in August 1861, was still being read and reflected on. Douglass compared Tillman to some of the black heroes of the past, rebels for freedom such as the South Carolina slave rebel Denmark Vesey, the Virginia slave rebel Nat Turner, and the Haitian revolutionary Toussaint Louverture, proclaiming (with an allusion to Shakespeare's Mark Antony) that Tillman "walked to his work of self-deliverance with a step as firm and dauntless as the noblest Roman of them all. . . . Well done for TILLMAN!" Douglass intoned, before closing with the searching questions: "When will this nation cease to disparage the negro race? When will they become sensible of the force of this irresistible TILLMAN argument?"[25]

In 1864, while the war was still raging, a rousing retelling of Tillman's story was published in Philadelphia in a book titled *The Bugle Blast; or Spirit of the Conflict*. Culled almost entirely from published newspaper accounts, the story appeared under the heading "Tragedy of the Schooner S. J. Waring," although the author, a staunch pro-Unionist named E. S. S. Rouse, made it clear that Tillman was "the hero of it."[26]

In 1865, a Philadelphia publishing house issued a small paperbound book that included a lurid account of the Tillman story. Titled *The Rebel Pirate's Fatal Prize; or, the Bloody Tragedy of the Prize Schooner Waring*, it purported to be based on "the life and confessions of the steward, William Tillman, the brave and daring Negro, who, with a hatchet, murdered the rebel prize master, lieutenant, and mate, whom he overheard secretly plotting to sell him into slavery, recaptured the vessel, and brought her into a free port." The same book included "the thrilling history of Hope Carter, the mulatto contraband and Tennessee slave, together with the sinking of the rebel privateer, *Petrel*, by the U.S. Frigate, *St. Lawrence*, the Capture of *Jeff Davis* and the *Enchantress*, and trial of the rebel pirates." Tillman's story was supposedly told by a "passenger of the *Waring* and an eye witness to the bloody scenes," but neither the passenger nor the eyewitness was named. The writer apparently preferred to remain anonymous—no one is credited with authorship—for the book included lots of fiction and invention totally unrelated to the actual facts of Tillman's story. Hope Carter was identified as Tillman's wife, and Tillman was said to have taken an early voyage up the Mississippi from New Orleans in a steamer that "struck hard upon a snag" and broke "asunder, a complete wreck." Of course these assertions were wholly fabricated, as was the charge that Tillman "murdered" the Confederate prize officers. Hope Carter was not his wife; Tillman was, so far as the available evidence reveals, never employed on the Mississippi; and he was never charged with, much less convicted of, "murder" but was instead celebrated for his shipboard heroism.[27]

A former slave from Kentucky named William Wells Brown published the first history of black military participation in the Civil War in 1867. Recognized as an accomplished writer and speaker, Brown included a chapter titled "Heroism of Negroes on the High Seas" in his *The Negro in the American Rebellion*. It included an account of Tillman's rescue of the *S. J. Waring* that misstated some of the details of Tillman's story: It said that the schooner was captured in June instead of July 1861, that the privateers put one of the Yankees aboard in irons, that Tillman attacked the Confederate officers with a club instead of

with a hatchet, and that after Tillman returned to New York
he received an "award" from the federal government instead
of a court-ordered salvage payment from the owners of the
Waring and its cargo. But Brown quoted the *New York Tribune*
as having endorsed Tillman's heroism by writing: "To this colored man was the nation indebted for the first vindication of
its honor on the sea."[28]

The famous black educator Booker T. Washington published a book appraising African American accomplishments
in 1900. His *A New Negro for a New Century: An Accurate and
Up-to-Date Record of the Upward Struggle of the Negro Race*
included two pages about Tillman's recapture of the *S. J. Waring* that repeated errors in William Wells Brown's account but
nonetheless credited Tillman with real heroism. Detailing the
threat of the privateers to take Tillman to a Southern slave
auction, Washington wrote that "the Negro was as brave as a
lion, and resolved that the ship should never reach Charleston.
With him to resolve was to act."[29]

Although evidence as to whether William Tillman played
any part in the fighting that followed his reception as a hero
in New York is distressingly thin, it appears that he did not.
There is good documentation that he registered for the draft in
June 1863. He had by that time returned to his home in Providence, Rhode Island, where he was listed in the enrollment
records as a twenty-nine-year-old "colored seaman" living at
29 C Street in Rhode Island's First Congressional District.
His full name was given in this listing as "William B. Till-

man."[30] But there is no record that he ever served in either the army or the navy. This does not suggest that he was a shirker, for many able-bodied men—prominent whites as well as humble blacks—saw no military service during the Civil War.[31] Tillman had already seen combat aboard the *S. J. Waring* and risked his life to escape being sold into slavery. He had already proved his bravery and heroism and may not have felt the need to do so a second time.

Perhaps Tillman was able to pay the three-hundred-dollar commutation fee provided for in the conscription law. Many men in the North did just that during the war. They were usually men of means—three hundred dollars was a substantial sum at that time—but Tillman had received a large salvage award for saving the *S. J. Waring* and may have been able to use some of that money to pay the fee.[32] We do know that by the time the draft was decreed Tillman was a married man and had other obligations, for the Rhode Island marriage records show that he married a woman named Julia A. Prophet on January 15, 1863.[33] "William B. Tillman" was listed in the Providence City Directory for 1864 as a "boatman" living at 29 C. Street.[34] The Rhode Island State Census for 1865 shows that William B. Tillman, then thirty, and Julia A. Tillman, twenty-one, were living in Cranston Township in Providence. He was a black mariner and she was a black housekeeper.[35] The U.S. Census for 1870 provides some additional information. It lists William B. Tillman, a black sailor, living in Cranston Township, with Julia Tillman, a black housekeeper, and a one-year-old child named Frederick Tillman. The child was born in Rhode Island.[36]

The last records that tell us anything about the hero of the *S. J. Waring* are as scanty as the rest. They are the 1880 city directory for far-off San Francisco, California, and the federal census records of 1880 for the same city. These reveal that a black cook named William Tillman was then living as a boarder at 115 Second Street in the California city. He was divorced, but neither the cause nor the date of the divorce are hinted at. He had a health problem of some sort—perhaps a "sore eye"—but its precise nature is impossible to make out because the handwritten records are illegible.[37]

Tillman's illiteracy is a good explanation for the absence of any letters, diaries, or memoirs in his own hand. In that respect Tillman was no different from millions of his fellow blacks in the nineteenth century—and no different from millions of whites who lived in poverty and obscurity and, like William Stedding and Donald McLeod, could not even scribble their own names.

Although it is frustratingly difficult to trace even the basic facts of William Tillman's life after he was acclaimed as a hero of the Civil War, it is easier to review the fates of the ships that played so prominent a part in his story.

The *Jefferson Davis*'s life as a Confederate privateer was exciting but ultimately destined to be short. July 6, 1861, the day before it captured the *S. J. Waring* outside New York, proved to be its most active, for that same day it also captured the brig *John Welsh* from Philadelphia and the schooner *Enchantress* from Boston. Not knowing the fate of the prize officers who were put aboard the *Waring*, the *Davis*'s officers continued to prowl the ocean as far north as Rhode Island and as far south as Puerto Rico, capturing some valuable Yankee merchantmen and seizing some others that it quickly decided to release because they were not suitable to be taken as prizes. It also burned at least one vessel at sea. In all the *Davis* captured or destroyed eight vessels.[38] Then, on Friday, August 16, exactly six weeks after its departure from the harbor of Charleston, it found itself in distress off the coast of northeast Florida. All the crew members who were suitable for service as prize officers had been put aboard captured vessels, and the *Davis*'s provisions and water were running dangerously low. Captain Coxetter attempted to pilot the privateer through an opening in the bar that lay between St. Augustine and the open sea, but the wind was blowing so hard he could not make it. He waited until Sunday, August 18, and then tried again to navigate the bar. But the wind was still blowing so badly that the *Jeff Davis* ran aground. Desperate, Coxetter threw some of his heavy guns overboard, but even this did not enable the beleaguered vessel to move. Boats from the harbor had witnessed the privateer's struggle and came out to take the officers and crew ashore. When they reached St. Augustine, they were greeted with cheers from the townspeople. Two weeks later, Coxetter went by train to Charleston, where he was greeted by admirers and presented with a gold watch. The *Charleston*

Daily Mercury exulted: "The name of the privateer *Jefferson Davis* has become a word of terror to the Yankees. The number of her prizes and the amount of merchandise which she captured have no parallel since the days of the *Saucy Jack* (a Charleston schooner renowned as one of the most successful privateers in the War of 1812).[39]

Although its crew was rescued, the *Jeff Davis* sank into the sea. Nearly a century and a half later, marine archaeologists attempted to locate the wreck but were unable to do so. Their efforts were the subject of a documentary film that was screened as part of the Orlando Film Festival and at the Museum of Florida History in Tallahassee in 2011.[40]

Despite its short life and unhappy death, the *Jeff Davis* was actually the most successful of all the Confederate privateers.[41] In total there were only about a dozen of the secessionist marauders, and their captures came to only about twenty-seven merchant ships.[42] Their exploits were daring and dramatic, to be sure, but they did not contribute much to the Southern war effort.[43] The prizes they took into Confederate ports carried valuable cargoes, but the vessels themselves were not really useful to the Confederate navy. They were slow—the ability of the privateers to catch them was evidence of that—and they were poorly suited to combat.[44] And because other nations would not allow captured prizes to be brought into their ports—Nassau, Bermuda, or Havana, for example—the privateers were forced to try to take them into Southern harbors.[45] This sometimes required them to make desperate efforts to elude the blockading ships of the Union navy. Bowing to reality, the Confederates decided to rely more on blockade runners—ships that were designed for speed and the ability to slip through the Union blockade, delivering cargoes of needed ordnance and supplies to the South and taking out its own products, mostly cotton and other agricultural products—and on raiders, specially constructed ships operated by the Confederate navy and equipped to capture Yankee vessels.

In contrast to the *Jefferson Davis*, the *S. J. Waring*'s life as a profitable merchant vessel continued for years after the Civil War. As soon as the U.S. marshal's attachment was released, the schooner was returned to Jonas Smith's management, where it continued to sail the open seas and along the Southern coastline, wary always of the dangers it might encounter.

Bryce MacKinnon's testimony in the salvage trial showed that the *Waring* promptly completed the voyage to South America that was interrupted by the *Jefferson Davis*, thereby delivering its valuable cargo to Montevideo and Buenos Aires.[46] Union navy records reveal that, in July 1862, it was off the coast of South Carolina when it took on a valuable cargo of rice that a blockading vessel had seized from a Confederate transport ship, and took it to New York as a prize capture.[47]

The *Waring* was about two hundred miles north of Matanilla Reef in the Bahamas in October 1866, when it picked up some of the survivors of a devastating hurricane. The steamship *Evening Star*, carrying some 270 passengers, had sunk in the storm, and only seventeen of the passengers survived. They were first rescued by the *Fleetwing*, a Norwegian bark bound for Southampton, England, but when the *Waring* came on the scene it agreed to take them to Savannah. Safely transported to the Georgia city—no longer in Confederate hands—the survivors spoke of the "many kindnesses" they received from the captain of the *Fleetwing* and "from Captain Smith, of the *Waring*, for which we are most grateful."[48]

Jonas Smith continued to operate his fleet of vessels from his New York headquarters for two years after the end of the war. His death in 1867, and the large estate he left of ships and real estate in and around Stony Brook, Long Island, earned him the name of "Rich Jonas," by which the locals remembered him. He was survived by a widow but no children. His will included a generous bequest of eight thousand dollars to build a school. Bearing the name Smithtown Academy, the school was adorned with a handsome plaque inscribed:

> To the memory of Jonas Smith, the founder, and his esteemed widow, Nancy Smith, the patron, these halls are dedicated. Without opportunity of education, or assistance from friends in youth, he was the architect of his own fortune; far-seeing, clearly-discerning, soundly-judging, and promptly-deciding, he marked whatever he touched; a pattern of sobriety, integrity and industry, he wanted only the polish of education to make him a perfect man. He leaves this legacy to you, pupils, that you may here enjoy, in early life, the privileges which were denied to him.[49]

According to the recollections of a Stony Brook man whose father managed the Jonas Smith shipping company after Smith's death, the *S. J. Waring* continued to sail into the 1880s. By then it was destined to be put to rest, for three decades of useful service had taken their toll on the old wooden ship, weakening its timbers, warping and cracking its planking, and twisting its masts and spars. And by the 1880s steam-powered ships and ironclad hulls were replacing oaken vessels almost everywhere. So the *Waring* was towed to Stony Brook Harbor and beached. There the schooner "gradually went to pieces where she lay," and half a century later its keels and ribs were "buried deep in the shifting sands on the bottom of the harbor."[50]

A BLACK MAN'S FATE

Sadly, no answers to the questions of what happened to William Tillman after 1880, where he lived, how he made his living, and when and where he died, have been found. The historian Gerald S. Henig, a close student of Tillman's story, has written that, after Tillman's salvage award was affirmed on appeal to the U.S. Circuit Court in New York, he "vanishes from the historical radar screen. In spite of exhaustive research, no verifiable evidence has turned up to document his later years."[1]

Of course William Tillman was not the only hero of the Civil War who all but disappeared after the great conflict ended. He was not the only black man who showed great bravery during the struggle only to fall into obscurity in the years that followed. Nor was he the only African American whose wartime bravery helped to bring slavery in the United States to an end.

One of the most notable men who was also recognized as a hero of the war was Robert Smalls, a twenty-three-year-old slave from Beaufort, South Carolina. Smalls was employed as a pilot on a Confederate steamer in the harbor of Charleston

in May 1862, eight months after Tillman's recapture of the
S. J. Waring, when he and seven other slaves managed to steer
the steamer out from under the noses of Confederate fortifications and deliver it to a Union vessel waiting outside the
harbor entrance.[2] The steamer was the *Planter*, a well-armed
dispatch and transportation vessel attached to the engineer-
ing department at Charleston. The Confederate captain and
mates had left it unattended, and in the early morning hours of
May 13, the slaves, led by Smalls, loaded their families aboard
and navigated it under the guns of the forts then guarding
the harbor (including Fort Sumter), saluting them with their
steam whistle as they passed by. When they reached the open
sea, they flagged down the first blockading vessel they could
find and turned the steamer over to the Union navy.[3] The officers who received the *Planter* were impressed by the vessel,
which was quickly put into Union service, and by Smalls, who
was praised as a "quite intelligent" slave who not only brought
them a valuable vessel with valuable armaments aboard but
also gave them "some valuable information" about Confederate activities in Charleston.[4] Smalls received official recognition when, only two weeks after his capture of the steamer,
President Lincoln signed an act of Congress ordering that the
Planter be appraised as a prize of war and that half its value be
divided among Smalls and the other slaves who helped him.
The *Planter*'s value was eventually set at nine thousand dollars and Smalls's share at fifteen hundred.[5] After this official
recognition, Smalls went on to render important service as a

pilot of Union army boats that ran up and down the Southern coastline and took part in some seventeen naval battles.[6] Most notably, after the war concluded, and with Union troops occupying South Carolina to ensure that black civil rights would be respected, Smalls commenced an active political career that included election to both the South Carolina legislature and the U.S. Congress, and an appointment as a major general of the South Carolina state militia.[7]

Yet millions of Smalls's fellow blacks survived only to live out their lives in the dark shadows cast over the nation by the great national tragedy. The bloody fighting between the North and the South came to an end in the spring of 1865, almost four years after William Tillman brought the schooner *S. J. Waring* back from its Confederate captivity to New York. The heroism that began with Tillman's bold rescue of the schooner had borne fruit in the recapture of the defiant Confederate states by armies of whites and blacks loyal to the Union. Tillman had escaped the clutches of slavery, preserving his own freedom, and some four million black slaves were now within sight of the final end of slavery.

Republicans dedicated to the preservation of the Union and the abolition of slavery were now in control of the U.S. Congress. After extensive—and oftentimes bitter—debates, they were able to approve three monumental amendments to the U.S. Constitution and send them to the states for ratification. The Thirteenth Amendment, ratified on December 6, 1865, ended slavery, providing that "neither slavery nor involuntary servitude, except as a punishment for crime whereof the party shall have been duly convicted, shall exist within the United States, or any place subject to their jurisdiction."[8] The Fourteenth Amendment, ratified on July 9, 1868, contained two bold statements of expanded civil rights. The first was that "all persons born or naturalized in the United States, and subject to the jurisdiction thereof, are citizens of the United States and of the state wherein they reside." The second was that "no state shall make or enforce any law which shall abridge the privileges or immunities of citizens of the United States, nor shall any state deprive any person of life, liberty, or property, without due process of law; nor deny to any person within its jurisdiction the equal protection of the laws."[9] These provisions clearly abolished the old rules (proclaimed most boldly in the Supreme Court's 1857 decision in *Dred Scott v. Sandford*)[10] that persons of African ancestry were not eligible for citizenship, and that despised minorities (African Americans chief among them) could be discriminated against with impunity. The Fifteenth Amendment, ratified on February 3, 1870, added a further emphatic statement that "the right of citizens of the United States to vote shall not be denied or abridged by the United States or by any state on account of race, color, or previous condition of servitude."[11]

In 1865 Congress established a Bureau of Refugees, Freedman, and Abandoned Lands, popularly known as the Freedmen's Bureau, to help former slaves establish themselves under the new rules of freedom.[12] It provided food, housing, medical aid, and legal assistance to needy blacks. It also established schools for African Americans and tried to settle them on Confederate lands that had been confiscated or abandoned during the war. In 1866, Congress passed a civil rights act, granting the same civil rights enjoyed by white citizens to all male persons in the United States "without distinction of race or color, or previous condition of slavery or involuntary servitude."[13] U.S. Army troops were sent to Southern states to monitor and enforce the new rules of freedom, to provide food, clothing, and medical care to former slaves, and also destitute whites.

The Freedmen's Bureau continued its work until it was dismantled in 1872. For a while blacks were actually permitted to vote, to elect representatives, and to purchase their own lands. This period, known as Reconstruction, persisted until 1877, when a fierce contest over the disputed results of the 1876 presidential election forced the removal of the U.S. troops and a return to the old ways of racial discrimination. Freed from supervision, former slaveholding states enacted laws designed to keep blacks out of the way of whites, to prevent them from voting, and to deny them good educations. Rigid rules of segregation were adopted. Literacy tests were devised to keep men who had been systematically barred from learning to read or write out of the polling places. Poll taxes were imposed, while hooded mobs roamed the countryside with ropes ready to hang resistant blacks from the overhanging branches of trees. And so African Americans were returned to their assigned places. They were no longer subject to legally enforced slavery, but they were subject to the strictures of Jim Crow. Even Robert Smalls's postwar career was ended by the advent of Jim Crow, literacy tests, and poll taxes.[14]

History is a great intellectual discipline, a repository of shared memory, and a sometimes inspired branch of literature. But it is also a hard taskmaster. The great cynic Ambrose Bierce acerbically defined history as "an account mostly false, of events mostly unimportant, which are brought about by rulers mostly knaves, and soldiers mostly fools."[15] The American historian Frederick Jackson Turner wrote that "history, both objective and subjective, is ever becoming, never completed,"[16] while the American artist and philosopher Elbert Hubbard called history a mere "collection of epitaphs."[17]

If William Tillman left an epitaph, we do not know where or how it was recorded. We do not know where he died, where he was buried, or even if his burial place was marked. We know that he survived the Civil War in the long shadows left by that terrible conflict, a man unnoticed and forgotten. But we also know that he demonstrated courage, valor, and determination at the beginning of the war, that he was recognized then as a hero—the first real hero of the conflict—and that his heroism was followed by the similar heroism of countless other blacks in the years that followed. That knowledge alone should be enough to reawaken our interest in his story.

ACKNOWLEDGMENTS

The heart of this book is, of course, the research that helped me track down the facts about William Tillman's Civil War heroism and the compelling circumstances that make his story worth retelling today. I am grateful to many individuals who responded to my requests for books, articles, pamphlets, judicial archives, newspaper files, images, and other materials that enabled me to put flesh on the bones of a story that commanded my attention when I first encountered it and still fascinates me. And so I offer my thanks to Peter Bae, Tara C. Craig, and Emily Holmes of the Butler Library at Columbia University; Lisa Schoblasky of the Newberry Library in Chicago; Patrick Connelly of the National Archives in Philadelphia; Gregory J. Plunges of the National Archives in New York City; Pamela J. Anderson of the National Archives in Kansas City; Robert Delap of the New-York Historical Society; Kristen J. Nitray of the Frank Melville Jr. Memorial Library at Stony Brook University; Lauren Rasmussen of the San Diego History Center; Jessica Macfarlane of the National Maritime Historical Society in Peekskill, New York; Ed Richi of the Delaware Historical Society in Wilmington; Mark Murphy of the Morris Library at the University of Delaware in Newark; Carol Heller of the Kent State University Press in Kent, Ohio; and Karen Martin, archivist of the Three Village Historical Society in East Setauket, New York. Thanks are also due my agent, Matthew Carnicelli, for his guidance, and Phil Marino, my editor at Liveright, for his skillful editing. Jim Barnett was involved in the planning and execution of the book from the start, helping with the research, listening to me explain my ideas and giving me his comments on them, reviewing the manuscript and spotting errors. He has my sincere thanks. I wish to express special appreciation to Gerald S. Henig, Emeritus Professor of History at

California State University, East Bay, who has studied William Tillman for many years and at one time hoped to write his own book about Tillman's heroism. When I informed him that I was about to write Tillman's story in this book, he readily agreed to review the manuscript and offer his comments and corrections. Any errors that persist in the text are, of course, my responsibility alone.

NOTES

PROLOGUE

1 Debates among historians about what "caused" the Civil War have been long and persistent. The many answers given to this troubling question seem to me to depend in large part on the questions that precede it. If one asks "What caused the Civil War?" a multitude of possible answers suggest themselves. One person might answer: "It was President Lincoln's call for 75,000 volunteers to come to Washington and defend the capital against anticipated military attack." "No," another might argue, "it was the Confederate bombardment of Fort Sumter in Charleston Harbor—the first use of military power in the long-brewing conflict between the sections." "No," yet another might say, "it was President Lincoln's effort to resupply Fort Sumter before the Confederate bombardment began." "No," still another person might counter, "it was the secession of the slaveholding states of the Deep South and the formation of the Confederate States of America." "No," someone else might declare, "it was the resistance to the Fugitive Slave Act of 1850 in various Northern States." "No," yet another person might insist, "it was John Brown's bloody raid on Harpers Ferry in 1859, an attack that aroused resentment and anger in the South and provoked abolitionist fury in the North." And so on. If, however, the question is "What was the Civil War about?" only one answer seems truly credible. It was about slavery, an institution that the South cherished for both its social and its economic importance to Southern institutions, and one that was coming under increasing criticism and attack in the North—and indeed in the rest of the world. Southerners who occupied positions of power in 1860 believed fer-

vently in the perpetuation, even the expansion, of slavery, while the Republican Party of Abraham Lincoln believed it should be brought to "ultimate extinction." (See Oakes, *Freedom National: The Destruction of Slavery in the United States, 1861–1865*, 1–48.) Lincoln's election convinced Southerners that under Republican leadership "ultimate extinction" would eventually occur. Lincoln himself expressed it most succinctly and cogently when, in his Second Inaugural Address, he stated that at the beginning of the war "one eighth of the whole population [of the United States] were colored slaves, not distributed generally over the Union, but localized in the Southern part of it. These slaves constituted a peculiar and powerful interest. All knew that this interest was, somehow, the cause of the war. To strengthen, perpetuate, and extend this interest was the object for which the insurgents would rend the Union, even by war." Basler, *Collected Works of Abraham Lincoln*, 8:332. As the historian James Oakes has stated: "The real moral dilemma of the Civil War, however, arises from the fact that it *was* about slavery." Oakes, *Freedom National: The Destruction of Slavery in the United States, 1861–1865*, xvi. The historian Edward L. Ayers has examined the question of what caused the Civil War with insight and erudition. Identifying many factors that played a part in the growing tensions that erupted in war in 1861, he has concluded that slavery was at the heart of them. "What caused the Civil War?" Ayers has asked. "If you have to offer a one-word answer, go ahead and just say slavery. But you should know what you mean by that answer." See Ayers, *What Caused Slavery?*, 142.

2   The U.S. Constitution, Article I, Section 9, forbade Congress from prohibiting the slave trade before 1808, and Article V forbade any amendment to this provision before 1808. In 1807 Congress passed a law prohibiting the importation of slaves effective January 1, 1808. See 2 *Stat.* 426, "An act to prohibit the importation of slaves into any port or place within the jurisdiction of the United States, from and after the first day of January, in the year of our Lord one thousand eight hundred and eight," March 2, 1807. Some earlier statutes had restricted American participation in the international slave trade. See Fehrenbacher, *The Slaveholding Republic*, 43, 148.

3   It is not the purpose of this book to acquaint readers with the grim realities of slavery in the United States in the middle of the nine-

teenth century, as many readers will already be familiar with them. Since William Tillman was an African American, however, since he was born and lived all of his life as a free man, and since he was credibly threatened with being sold into Southern slavery when he was captured by Confederate privateers in July 1861, it is impossible to totally avoid some discussion of the "peculiar institution" and the facts that made Tillman so resistant to the threat of being subjected to it.

4   "Negro and White Population of the United States in 1860 (Compiled from the Census Returns of 1860)," in McPherson, *The Negro's Civil War*, appendix A.

5   Minutes of Testimony, *William Tillman and others v. The Schooner S. J. Waring, her tackle, apparel, furniture, and cargo*, U.S. District Court, Southern District of New York.

6   The Civil War historian Gerald S. Henig, who has probably devoted more time and effort to the study of William Tillman than any other scholar, has written that, despite exhaustive research, no verifiable information about Tillman's later years has been found. See Henig, "The Union's First Black Hero: William Tillman," 84. See also discussion in chapter 8.

ONE: A FREE BLACK MAN

1   In October 1861, Tillman testified that he was born in Milford in Delaware and that he was twenty-seven years old. Minutes of Testimony, *William Tillman and others v. The Schooner S. J. Waring, her tackle, apparel, furniture, and cargo*, U.S. District Court, Southern District of New York.

2   Davis, *Inhuman Bondage*, 125. See Gates, "Who Was the First African American?" http://www.theroot.com/articles/history/2012/10/who_was_the_first_african_american_100_amazing_facts_about_the_negro.html.

3   Essah, *A House Divided*, 9–10, 15; Williams, *Slavery and Freedom in Delaware*, 6–7.

4   Essah, *A House Divided*, 9, 13; Williams, *Slavery and Freedom in Delaware*, xv, 2–3.

5   Williams, *Slavery and Freedom in Delaware*, 2–3.

6   Ibid., 4.

7   Davis, *The Problem of Slavery in the Age of Emancipation*, 245; Davis, *Inhuman Bondage*, xiv.

8   Williams, *Slavery and Freedom in Delaware*, 11–12, 33–34, 45; Essah, *A House Divided*, 10, 26–32, 37.

9   Williams, *Slavery and Freedom in Delaware*, 249.

10   Ibid., 187.

11   Ibid., 155.

12   Henig, "William Tillman, the Union's First Black Hero," 81.

13   Hancock, "Not Quite Men," 320–322; Henig, "William Tillman: The Union's First Black Hero," 81; Williams, *Freedom and Slavery in Delaware*, 37, 145.

14   Williams, *Slavery and Freedom in Delaware*, 70–71.

15   Ibid., 249–250; Hancock, "Not Quite Men: The Free Negroes in Delaware in the 1830's," 320.

16   Williams, *Slavery and Freedom in Delaware*, xvi–xvii.

17   Davis, *Inhuman Bondage*, 152; Davis, *The Problem of Slavery in the Age of Emancipation*, 244.

18   Davis, *The Problem of Slavery in the Age of Emancipation*, 244, 245, 271.

19   Hancock, "Not Quite Men: The Free Negroes in Delaware in the 1830's," 322.

20   Davis, *The Problem of Slavery in the Age of Emancipation*, 245. See U.S. Const., Art. 1, Sec. 2 (representation in House of Representatives to include "the whole number of free persons" plus "three fifths of all other persons"); Art. 1, Sec. 9, cl. 1 (slave trade not to be prohibited before year 1808); Art. 4, Sec. 2, cl. 3 (return of fugitive slaves).

21   Litwack, *North of Slavery*, 4.

22   Davis, *Inhuman Bondage*, 152.

23   Litwack, *North of Slavery*, 14–15.

24   Williams, *Slavery and Freedom in Delaware*, 187–188.

25   Davis, *The Problem of Slavery in the Age of Emancipation*, 78, 204–205, 209, 249, 271–272, 387n23; Davis, *Inhuman Bondage*, 157–174, 186, 208–209, 222–226, 259, 381nn12, 14, 15, 17.

26   Williams, *Slavery and Freedom in Delaware*, 220.

27   Ibid., 203.

28   Federal Census for 1800, Murderkill Hundred, Kent County, Delaware.

29 Delaware Marriage Records, 1744–1912, Dover, Delaware: Delaware Public Archives, Records Group RG 1325, Subgroup 003, Series 004.

30 Federal Census for 1840, Dover Hundred, Kent County, Delaware.

31 Federal Census for 1850, Dover Hundred, Kent County, Delaware.

32 Federal Census for 1850, Wilmington, New Castle County, Delaware.

33 *The Emancipator*, August 5, 1837, and *The Colored American*, August 12, 1837.

34 Hancock, "William Yates's Letter of 1837: Slavery and Colored People in Delaware," 208.

35 Williams, *Slavery and Freedom in Delaware*, 201–207.

36 Ibid., 202–207; Essah, *A House Divided*, 140–145.

37 James E. Newton, "Black Americans in Delaware: An Overview."

38 Essah, *A House Divided*, 137–138.

39 Williams, *Slavery and Freedom in Delaware*, 207–208; Essah, *A House Divided*, 138.

40 Williams, *Slavery and Freedom in Delaware*, 207.

41 Ibid., 207–208.

42 Ibid., 162–176.

43 Laws of the State of Delaware, 10:414–416; Williams, *Slavery and Freedom in Delaware*, 197; Essah, *A House Divided*, 137.

44 Williams, *Slavery and Freedom in Delaware*, xiii.

45 Testimony of William Tillman, Minutes of Testimony, *William Tillman and others v. The Schooner S. J. Waring, her tackle, apparel, furniture, and cargo*, U.S. District Court, Southern District of New York; Henig, "William Tillman: The Union's First Black Hero," 81.

46 Litwack, *North of Slavery*, 34–39, 70–74.

47 Cottrol, *The Afro-Yankees*, 17.

48 Bolster, *Black Jacks*, 27; Fehrenbacher, *The Slaveholding Republic*, 135, 140.

49 Gradual Emancipation Act of March 1, 1784; Litwack, *North of Slavery*, 3n1; Cottrol, *The Afro-Yankees*, 14, 16.

50 Cottrol, *The Afro-Yankees*, 29.

51 Bolster, *Black Jacks*, 7–43.

52 Williams, *Slavery and Freedom in Delaware*, 68.

53 Testimony of William Tillman, Minutes of Testimony, *William Tillman and others v. The Schooner S. J. Waring, her tackle, apparel, furniture, and cargo*, U.S. District Court, Southern District of New York.

54 This description was printed in "The Negro William Tillman," *New York Herald*, July 22, 1861, 5. A contemporaneous description in "The Story of Wm. Tillman, the Steward," *New York Daily Tribune*, July 22, 1861, 8, reads: "He is of medium hight [sic], rather strongly built, crisp hair, of nearly unmixed negro blood."

TWO: TO SEA

1 Minutes of Testimony, *William Tillman and others v. The Schooner S. J. Waring, her tackle, apparel, furniture, and cargo*, U.S. District Court, Southern District of New York.

2 Bolster, *Black Jacks*, 2.

3 Henig, "William Tillman: The Union's First Black Hero," 81; Bolster, *Black Jacks*, 167.

4 Bolster, *Black Jacks*, 70–81.

5 Farr, *Black Odyssey*, 56.

6 Dana, *The Seaman's Friend*, 156.

7 Bolster, *Black Jacks*, 33, 168.

8 Bayles, *Historical and Descriptive Sketches of Suffolk County and Its Towns, Villages, Hamlets, Scenery, Institutions and Important Enterprises*, 239.

9 Three Village Historical Society, *Images of America: Stony Brook*, 73; Welch, *An Island's Trade*, 1.

10 *Brooklyn Daily Eagle*, September 29, 1895, 8, listing forty-four vessels owned by Jonas Smith, with the dates and places where they were built. Welch, *An Island's Trade*, 33, says that Stony Brook "remained a secondary shipbuilding center throughout the nineteenth century."

11 *Records of the Town of Brookhaven, Suffolk County, N.Y.*, 312–314, 332–334, 406–408; Three Village Historical Society, *Images of America: Stony Brook*, 77, 84, 92.

12 *Trow's New York City Directory for the Year Ending May 1, 1857*, 769; *Smith's Brooklyn Directory for the Year Ending May 1, 1857*, 277; *Brooklyn City Directory for the Year Ending May 1, 1858*, 342; *Brooklyn Daily Eagle*, June 26, 1860, 2; *Brooklyn City Directory for the Year Ending May 1, 1862*, 406; *Brooklyn City Directory for the Year Ending May 1, 1863*, 405.

13 *Brooklyn Daily Eagle*, September 29, 1895, 8. Due to a typographical

error the name of this vessel is given as *J. J. Waring*, but there is no doubt that it is the same vessel as the *S. J. Waring*.

14 Edward H. Davis, "Port Jefferson, L.I., 1946," in handwritten manuscripts and typescript, San Diego Historical Society, San Diego, California.

15 *American Lloyd's Registry of American and Foreign Shipping, 1859*, 426. Dana, *The Seaman's Friend*, 14, explains the amount a vessel will carry in proportion to its tonnage.

16 Edward H. Davis, "Port Jefferson, L.I., 1946," in handwritten manuscripts and typescript, San Diego Historical Society, San Diego, California.

17 *Trow's New York City Directory for the Year Ending May 1, 1860* (New York: John F. Long, Publisher), 26.

18 *The New-York City and Co-Partnership Directory for 1843 and 1844* (New York: John Doggett, Jr., 1843), 408; *Report of the Officers Constituting the Light-House Board.* 32nd Congress, 1st Sess., Ex. Doc. No. 28 (Washington, D.C., Printed by A. Boyd Hamilton, 1852), 36.

19 Edward H. Davis, "Port Jefferson, L.I., 1946," and "Story of the Schr. S. J. Waring," in handwritten manuscripts and typescript, San Diego Historical Society, San Diego, California.

20 Bolster, *Black Jacks*, 12.

21 Dana, *The Seaman's Friend*, 146.

22 See Bolster, *Black Jacks*, 11, 71, 72–73, 112–114. Richard Henry Dana's *Two Years Before the Mast*, a classic account of life at sea in the 1830s, contains many examples of the cruelty of a ship's captain and of the flogging he administered to crew members. See Dana, *Two Years Before the Mast*, 1:102–105, passim.

23 7 *Statutes at Large of South Carolina*, 461–462; see Bolster, *Black Jacks*, 194; Farr, *Black Odyssey*, 198.

24 Farr, *Black Odyssey*, 199.

25 Bolster, *Black Jacks*, 198–199.

26 McPherson, *Battle Cry of Freedom*, 264–274.

27 Basler, *Collected Works of Abraham Lincoln*, 4:331–332. On April 13 Lincoln told General in Chief Winfield Scott: "It does seem to me, general, that if I were Beauregard I would take Washington." Burlingame, *Abraham Lincoln: A Life*, 2:133.

28 McPherson, *Battle Cry of Freedom*, 274–275.

29 Burrows and Wallace, *Gotham*, 869.

30 McGinty, *The Body of John Merryman*, 43–46.

31 *Official Records of the Union and Confederate Navies*, series 2, vol. 3, 97–98.

32 Basler, *Collected Works of Abraham Lincoln*, 4:338–339. For a discussion of the long deliberative process that Lincoln engaged in before proclaiming the blockade, see McGinty, *Lincoln and the Court*, 121–125.

33 1 Stat. 112–117, "An Act for the Punishment of certain Crimes against the United States," April 30, 1790; 3 Stat. 510, "An Act to protect the commerce of the United States, and punish the crime of piracy," March 3, 1819; 3 Stat. 600–601, "An Act to continue in force 'An act to protect the commerce of the United States, and punish the crime of piracy,' and also to make further provision for punishing the crime of piracy," May 15, 1820. *Trial of the Officers and Crew of the Privateer Savannah, on the Charge of Piracy, in the United States Circuit Court for the Southern District of New York. Hon. Judges Nelson and Shipman, Presiding*, 1.

34 Robinson, *The Confederate Privateers* (a well-researched but very partisan text first published in 1928), 4, 12, echoes Jefferson Davis's views, saying that the Union attempt to hold Fort Sumter was an "act of war" similar to the German kaiser's invasion of Belgium in 1914. Lincoln's forces were "invaders" and "trespassers" violating the sovereign soil of South Carolina.

35 U.S. Const., art. I, sec. 8.

36 Confederate States Const., art. I, sec. 8.

37 Weitz, *The Confederacy on Trial*, 18; Fowler, *Under Two Flags: The American Navy in the Civil War*, 273–274.

38 *Conventions and Declarations between the Powers Concerning War, Arbitration and Neutrality* (The Hague: Martinus Nijhoff, 1915); Neff, *Justice in Blue and Gray*, 22–23; Robinson, *The Confederate Privateers*, 2.

39 Symonds, *The Civil War at Sea*, 7–8; McPherson, *War on the Waters*, 25.

40 Symonds, *The Civil War at Sea*, 17–18; McPherson, *War on the Waters*, 3, 27–29, 97.

41 Neff, *Justice in Blue and Gray*, 19, 21, 204–205.

42 *Conventions and Declarations between the Powers Concerning War, Arbitration and Neutrality*.

43 Neff, *Justice in Blue and Gray*, 175.

44 Basler, *Collected Works of Abraham Lincoln*, 4:346–347.

45 Wise, *Lifeline of the Confederacy*, 13; McPherson, *War on the Waters*, 25.

46 *Official Records of the Union and Confederate Navies*, series 2, vol. 3, 97–98.

47 Robinson, *The Confederate Privateers*, 15–16.

48 *Official Records of the Union and Confederate Navies*, series 2, vol. 3, 281–285; Robinson, *The Confederate Privateers*, 15–17.

49 Robinson, *The Confederate Privateers*, 18. See 2 Statutes at Large 759, "An act concerning Letters of Marque, Prizes, and Prize Goods," June 26, 1812; 2 Stat. 792, "An Act in addition to the act concerning letters of marque, prizes, and prize goods," January 27, 1813.

50 May 6, 1861, "An act recognizing the existence of war between the United States and the Confederate States; and concerning letters of marque, prizes and prize goods." See Robinson, *The Confederate Privateers*, 17–22.

51 Quoted in ibid., 30.

52 Ibid., 30.

53 Symonds, *The Civil War at Sea*, 78–79; Weitz, *The Confederacy on Trial*, 21–22; Robinson, *The Confederate Privateers*, 49–57.

54 *Official Records of the Union and Confederate Navies in the War of the Rebellion*, series 1, vol. 1, 42; series 2, vol. 1, 362–363, 364; Robinson, *The Confederate Privateers*, 59–62; "Doings of the Privateer Jeff. Davis," *New Orleans Daily Crescent*, August 2, 1861, 1. See also Turner, "The Search for the *Jefferson Davis* in the National Archives." http://www.staugustinelighthouse.org/LAMP/Historical_Research/the-search-for-the-jefferson-davis.

55 Robinson, *The Confederate Privateers*, 62; Weitz, *The Confederacy on Trial*, 23.

56 Quoted in Robinson, *The Confederate Privateers*, 62.

THREE: THE CAPTURE

1 *New Orleans Daily Crescent*, August 2, 1861.

2 Ibid.

3 Wells, "William Ross Postell, Adventurer," 395.

4 *New Orleans Daily Crescent*, August 2, 1861. See Wells, "William Ross

Postell, Adventurer," 398 (when he was on the *Davis,* Postell "was responsible to the captain for everything that happened aboard the vessel, and he relayed the captain's orders to officers and crew").

5   *Official Records of the Union and Confederate Navies in the War of the Rebellion,* series 2, vol. 1, 363.

6   Ibid., 363–364.

7   Wells, "William Ross Postell, Adventurer," 396, 404.

8   *Official Records of the Union and Confederate Navies in the War of the Rebellion,* series 2, vol. 1, 364–365.

9   Arrival of Recaptured Prizes," *New York Tribune,* July 22, 1861, 8.

10 "The Privateers," *New York Herald,* July 22, 1861, 4.

11 Robinson, *The Confederate Privateers,* 67; Chidsey, *The American Privateers,* 155.

12 Robinson, *The Confederate Privateers,* 67.

13 Scharf, *History of the Confederate States Navy,* 79; Robinson, *The Confederate Privateers,* 67–69; *Official Records of the Union and Confederate Navies in the War of the Rebellion,* series 1, vol. 1, 42.

14 "The Privateers," *New York Herald,* July 22, 1861, 4.

15 See *The Jeff Davis Piracy Cases: Full Report of the Trial of William Smith for Piracy, as One of the Crew of the Confederate Privateer, the Jeff Davis: Before Judges Grier and Cadwalader, in the Circuit Court of the United States, for the Eastern District of Pennsylvania, held at Philadelphia, in October, 1861,* 7–8, 11–13, 20, 24.

16 Scharf, *History of the Confederate States Navy,* 79; Robinson, *The Confederate Privateers,* 69; Chidsey, *The American Privateers,* 155.

17 "The Privateers," *New York Herald,* July 22, 1861, 4; Robinson, *The Confederate Privateers,* 81–84.

18 "A pilot is a person taken on board at a particular place for the purpose of conducting a ship through a river, road, or channel, or from or into a port. He is commonly appointed and licensed by public authority, and his compensation for services within the line of his ordinary duties, is usually fixed by law." Marvin, *A Treatise on the Law of Wreck and Salvage,* 152.

19 Spann, *Gotham at War,* 4.

20 Burrows and Wallace, *Gotham,* 865.

21 Ibid., 867–868; Spann, *Gotham at War,* 6.

22 Burrows and Wallace, *Gotham*, 858; Spann, *Gotham at War*, 121.

23 Burrows and Wallace, *Gotham*, 852–863.

24 Ibid., 868.

25 "Celebration of the Fourth," *New York Times*, July 6, 1861, 1.

26 "The Privateers," *New York Herald*, July 22, 1861, 4; Testimony of William Tillman in *William Tillman and others v. The Schooner S. J. Waring, her tackle, apparel, furniture, and cargo*, U.S. District Court, Southern District of New York.

27 See Dana, *The Seaman's Friend*, 133 ("Everything being in readiness, the customhouse and other regulations complied with, and the crew on board, the vessel is put under the charge of the pilot to be carried out clear of the land. While the pilot is on board, the master has little else to do than to see that everything is in order, and that the commands of the pilot are executed. As soon as the pilot leaves the ship, the entire control and responsibility is thrown upon the master").

28 Libel of William Tillman, William Stedding, and Donald McLeod, July 27, 1861, and Libel of Bryce MacKinnon, August 2, 1861, in *William Tillman and others v. The Schooner S. J. Waring, her tackle, apparel, furniture, and cargo*, U.S. District Court, Southern District of New York; "Marine Intelligence, New York, July 3," *New York Tribune*, July 4, 1861, 8.

29 Blunt, *The American Coast Pilot*, 18th ed., 32–52.

30 See "United States District Court[,] Southern District of New York," *New York Times*, December 24, 1861, 6 (opinion of Judge Shipman). Captain Francis Smith and Bryce MacKinnon were reported as having placed it at 38° 55′ north latitude and 69° west longitude. "Additional Particulars from Our Special Reporter," *New York Herald*, July 22, 1861, 4; "Narrative of Bryce MacKinnon, Passenger," *New York Tribune*, July 22, 1861, 8.

31 "Narrative of Bryce MacKinnon, Passenger," *New York Tribune*, July 22, 1861, 8.

32 "American vessels mostly have cotton sails, by which you can tell them very distinctively wherever you see them at sea[;] they are much whiter than hemp sails[;] all European vessels have hemp sails, and you can usually tell whether a vessel at sea is an American or foreign vessel by the sails, when you see nothing else." Testimony of John C. Fifield,

The Jeff Davis Piracy Cases: Full Report of the Trial of William Smith for Piracy, as One of the Crew of the Confederate Privateer, the Jeff Davis: Before Judges Grier and Cadwalader, in the Circuit Court of the United States, for the Eastern District of Pennsylvania, held at Philadelphia, in October, 1861, 31.

33   Ibid., 30, 31.

34   "Arrival of Recaptured Prizes," *New York Tribune*, July 22, 1861, 8.

35   Ibid.

36   Ibid.

37   Testimony of William Tillman, in *William Tillman and others v. The Schooner S. J. Waring, her tackle, apparel, furniture, and cargo*, U.S. District Court, Southern District of New York.

38   "Arrival of Recaptured Prizes," *New York Tribune*, July 22, 1861, 8.

39   Testimony of William Tillman, Minutes of Testimony, *William Tillman and others v. The Schooner S. J. Waring, her tackle, apparel, furniture, and cargo*, U.S. District Court, Southern District of New York; "Arrival of Recaptured Prizes," *New York Tribune*, July 22, 1861, 8.

40   "Arrival of Recaptured Prizes," *New York Tribune*, July 22, 1861, 8. Tillman later testified that Louis Coxetter, the captain of the *Jefferson Davis*, went into the cabin with Captain Smith and, after the papers were examined, "a bottle of brandy was called for & they drank." Testimony of William Tillman, in *William Tillman and others v. The Schooner S. J. Waring, her tackle, apparel, furniture, and cargo*, U.S. District Court, Southern District of New York. MacKinnon recalled that it was Postell who went into the cabin with Smith. MacKinnon's recollection seems more plausible.

41   "Arrival of Recaptured Prizes," *New York Tribune*, July 22, 1861, 8.

42   "The Privateers," *New York Herald*, July 22, 1861, 4.

43   Testimony of William Tillman, in *William Tillman and others v. The Schooner S. J. Waring, her tackle, apparel, furniture, and cargo*, U.S. District Court, Southern District of New York.

44   "The Privateers," *New York Herald*, July 22, 1861, 4.

45   "Additional Particulars from Our Special Reporters," ibid., 4.

46   "Arrival of Recaptured Prizes," *New York Tribune*, July 22, 1861, 8; *Official Records of the Union and Confederate Navies in the War of the Rebellion*, series 2, vol. 1, 364–365.

47   Seamen, both black and white, were confined aboard ship for long

periods and subject to severe discipline all the time. They called their leisure time "liberty." Bolster, *Black Jacks*, 70.

48 MacKinnon testified: "I was very sociable with them up to the time of the recapture. They treated me very kindly as a guest." Testimony of William Tillman, Minutes of Testimony, *William Tillman and others v. The Schooner S. J. Waring, her tackle, apparel, furniture, and cargo*, U.S. District Court, Southern District of New York.

49 "The Privateers," *New York Herald*, July 22, 1861, 4.

50 The proceeds of the sale were to be divided among the officers and crew members, according to the terms of their contract. See chapter 3.

51 "Arrival of Recaptured Prizes," *New York Tribune*, July 22, 1861, 8.

52 Testimony of William Tillman, in *William Tillman and others v. The Schooner S. J. Waring, her tackle, apparel, furniture, and cargo*, U.S. District Court, Southern District of New York.

53 "Arrival of Recaptured Prizes," *New York Tribune*, July 22, 1861, 8.

54 Ibid. The dialect recorded in this quotation may have come originally from MacKinnon, or it may simply have reflected the effort of the newspaper reporter to approximate black speech. It is printed here exactly as it appeared in the *New York Tribune*.

55 Testimony of William Tillman, Minutes of Testimony, in *William Tillman and others v. The Schooner S. J. Waring, her tackle, apparel, furniture, and cargo*, U.S. District Court, Southern District of New York.

56 "Arrival of Recaptured Prizes," *New York Tribune*, July 22, 1861, 8.

FOUR: NOW IS OUR TIME

1 Testimony of William Tillman, Minutes of Testimony, *William Tillman and others v. The Schooner S. J. Waring, her tackle, apparel, furniture, and cargo*, U.S. District Court, Southern District of New York. All the dialogue in this book is taken from original sources. None has been manufactured or embellished.

2 Testimony of William Stedding, Minutes of Testimony, ibid.

3 Testimony of William Tillman, ibid.

4 Ibid.

5 Ibid.

6 "United States District Court Southern District of New York," *New York Times*, December 24, 1861; Libel of Bryce MacKinnon in *William*

Tillman and others v. The Schooner S. J. Waring, her tackle, apparel, furniture, and cargo, August 2, 1861, U.S. District Court, Southern District of New York; Testimony of William Tillman, ibid.

7   Libel of Bryce MacKinnon, ibid.

8   Testimony of Bryce MacKinnon, Minutes of Testimony, ibid.; "Arrival of Recaptured Prizes," *New York Tribune*, July 22, 1861, 8.

9   Testimony of William Tillman, Minutes of Testimony, *William Tillman and others v. The Schooner S. J. Waring, her tackle, apparel, furniture, and cargo*, U.S. District Court, Southern District of New York.

10   Ibid. As described in "Notes on the Coast of the United States" by A. B. Bache, prepared for the use of blockading ships in 1861, the North Edisto River was "eighteen miles southwest of Charleston Bar and the first inlet of any value in a commercial point of view south of Charleston. It has more water than Charleston Bar—thirteen feet at mean low water, or nineteen feet at high water. The entrance is very direct, and vessels drawing not over twelve feet may enter safely on a single range."

11   Lincoln's blockade was initially proclaimed on April 19, 1861. On April 27, after the secession of Virginia and North Carolina, it was extended to cover those states. McPherson, *War on the Waters*, 20, 25; see Symonds, *The Civil War at Sea*, 40.

12   Testimony of William Tillman, Minutes of Testimony, *William Tillman and others v. The Schooner S. J. Waring, her tackle, apparel, furniture, and cargo*, U.S. District Court, Southern District of New York.

13   Testimony of Bryce MacKinnon, ibid.

14   Testimony of William Tillman, ibid.

15   Ibid.

16   Ibid.

17   Ibid.

18   Testimony of Bryce MacKinnon, ibid. MacKinnon testified that a "thrill of terror . . . like a touch of a battery" initially passed over him, but after he saw the state of affairs on the ship he "nerved himself up."

19   Ibid.

20   Testimony of William Tillman, ibid.

21   Ibid.

22   Testimony of William Tillman and Testimony of Bryce MacKinnon, ibid.

23   For a discussion of the claims later made in the court proceedings in New York that Tillman had acted in a "sanguinary" and unjustified manner, and the decision of U.S. District Judge William Shipman that he had responded appropriately to the "imminent and desperate" peril in which he found himself, see chapter 8.

24   Testimony of William Tillman, Minutes of Testimony, *William Tillman and others v. The Schooner S. J. Waring, her tackle, apparel, furniture, and cargo*, U.S. District Court, Southern District of New York. MacKinnon testified that Tillman "said, of course, he would shed as little blood as possible." Testimony of Bryce MacKinnon, Minutes of Testimony, ibid.

25   Dana, *Two Years Before the Mast*, 1:38.

FIVE: THE RETURN

1   "Arrival of Recaptured Prizes," *New York Tribune*, July 22, 1861, 8.

2   Libel of Bryce MacKinnon in *William Tillman and others v. The Schooner S. J. Waring, her tackle, apparel, furniture, and cargo*, U.S. District Court, Southern District of New York.

3   Although sextants and even quadrants are still used by navigators with an enthusiasm for antique instruments and methods, they have been almost entirely replaced by the Global Positioning System (GPS), a satellite-based navigation system.

4   Dana, *The Seaman's Friend*, 134, 145.

5   Ibid., 145.

6   Testimony of William Tillman, Minutes of Testimony, *William Tillman and others v. The Schooner S. J. Waring, her tackle, apparel, furniture, and cargo*, U.S. District Court, Southern District of New York ("There was no observation taken on board after the rescue, nor any reckoning").

7   Testimony of Bryce MacKinnon, ibid.

8   Testimony of William Tillman, ibid.

9   Testimony of William Tillman and Testimony of Bryce MacKinnon, ibid.

10   Testimony of Bryce MacKinnon, ibid.

11   Testimony of William Tillman, ibid.

12   The "fore peak" (sometimes called the "peak") of a vessel's hull was

the most forward part of the hold, just aft of the bow. It was small and confined and probably the most miserable part of the vessel to sail in. Seamen were sometimes held (or "shut down") there as punishment for serious offenses. See Dana, *Two Years Before the Mast*, 1:40.

13 Testimony of Bryce MacKinnon, Minutes of Testimony, in *William Tillman and others v. The Schooner S. J. Waring, her tackle, apparel, furniture, and cargo*, U.S. District Court, Southern District of New York.

14 Ibid.

15 See Dana, *The Seaman's Friend*, 133–134.

16 Testimony of William Tillman, Minutes of Testimony, *William Tillman and others v. The Schooner S. J. Waring, her tackle, apparel, furniture, and cargo*, U.S. District Court, Southern District of New York.

17 Testimony of William Tillman and Bryce MacKinnon, ibid.

18 Testimony of William Stedding, ibid.

19 Testimony of Bryce MacKinnon, ibid.

20 Testimony of William Tillman and Bryce MacKinnon, ibid.

21 Testimony of Bryce MacKinnon, ibid.

22 "The Privateers," *New York Herald*, July 22, 1861, 4.

23 "The Capture of the Schooner S. J. Waring. To the Editor of the Herald, Portland, Me., July 11, 1861," *New York Herald*, July 15, 1861, 2; Robinson, *The Confederate Privateers*, 70–71; Weitz, *The Confederacy on Trial*, 26.

24 Robinson, *The Confederate Privateers*, 71; Weitz, *The Confederacy on Trial*, 28; *Official Records of the Union and Confederate Navies in the War of the Rebellion*, series 1, vol. 1, 38.

25 *Official Records of the Union and Confederate Navies in the War of the Rebellion*, series 1, vol. 1, 38–39.

26 Ibid.; "Search for the Privateer Jeff. Davis," *New York Herald*, July 14, 1861, 1. Revenue cutters are official vessels authorized to enforce customs regulations and tariff laws.

27 "The Rebellion on the Ocean," *New York Herald*, July 15, 1861, 1.

28 Robinson, *The Confederate Privateers*, 73–74; Weitz, *The Confederacy on Trial*, 30–31.

29 Wise, *Lifeline of the Confederacy*, 13.

30 Testimony of William Tillman, Minutes of Testimony, *William Tillman and others v. The Schooner S. J. Waring, her tackle, apparel, furniture, and cargo*, U.S. District Court, Southern District of New York ("I

can neither read nor write"). Tillman's signature on the documents in his court case was made only by an X.

31   Testimony of William Stedding, ibid. Like Tillman's, Stedding's signature on the documents in the court case was made only by an X.

32   Testimony of Donald McLeod, ibid. Like Tillman's and Stedding's, McLeod's signature on the documents in the court case was made only by an X.

33   Blunt, *The American Coast Pilot*, 18th ed. (1857), title page. In the court testimony he gave after his return to New York, MacKinnon was asked if he had consulted the seventeenth edition of this book (1854), which was present in the courtroom. He said he could not specifically recall which edition it was, but suggested that it was not the 1854 edition because he could not recognize passages he had read aboard the ship in that edition. I have used the eighteenth edition in the research for this book; it was the most recent edition published before the outbreak of the war.

34   Testimony of Bryce MacKinnon, Minutes of Testimony, *William Tillman and others v. The Schooner S. J. Waring, her tackle, apparel, furniture, and cargo*, U.S. District Court, Southern District of New York.

35   Ibid.

36   Testimony of William Tillman, ibid.

37   Blunt, *The American Coast Pilot*, 341.

38   Ibid., 323.

39   Ibid.

40   Testimony of William Tillman and Bryce MacKinnon, Minutes of Testimony, *William Tillman and others v. The Schooner S. J. Waring, her tackle, apparel, furniture, and cargo*, U.S. District Court, Southern District of New York.

41   Testimony of William Tillman, ibid.

42   Blunt, *The American Coast Pilot*, 306.

43   Testimony of William Tillman, Minutes of Testimony, *William Tillman and others v. The Schooner S. J. Waring, her tackle, apparel, furniture, and cargo*, U.S. District Court, Southern District of New York.

44   "Jeff. Davis' [*sic*] Privateers," *New York Times*, July 22, 1861, 1.

45   "The Schooner," *New York Tribune*, July 22, 1861, 8; "Additional Particulars from Our Special Reporter," *New York Herald*, July 22, 1861, 4.

46   Ibid.

SIX: A HERO'S WELCOME

1   "The Capture of the Schooner S. J. Waring. To the Editor of the Herald, Portland, Me., July 11, 1861," *New York Herald*, July 15, 1861, 2; "Additional Particulars from Our Special Reporter," *New York Herald*, July 22, 1861, 4.

2   "The Schooner," *New York Tribune*, June 22, 1861, 8.

3   "The Prisoners Dorset [*sic*] and Molman [*sic*]," *New York Herald*, July 22, 1861, 5.

4   "William Tillman, The Colored Steward of the S. J. Waring," *New York Herald*, July 23, 1861, 5; "The Schooner," New York Tribune, July 22, 1861, 8; "Jeff Davis' [*sic*] Privateers," *New York Times*, July 22, 1861, 1.

5   "The Situation," *New York Herald*, July 25, 1861, 4.

6   "William Tillman, The Colored Steward of the S. J. Waring," *New York Herald*, July 23, 1861, 5.

7   Ibid. The questions and answers given by Tillman on this occasion have been copied directly from the newspaper account. They were written in more literate language than Tillman must have used, but they are included here because the reporters' account is far more informative than any speculation about what was said could have been.

8   Ibid.

9   "The Story of Wm. Tillman, the Steward," *New York Tribune*, July 22, 1861, 8.

10 "William Tillman, The Colored Steward of the S. J. Waring," *New York Herald*, July 23, 1861, 5.

11 "The Privateers in New York," *New York Times*, July 23, 1861, 6.

12 "William Tillman, The Colored Steward of the S. J. Waring," *New York Herald*, July 23, 1861, 5.

13 Ibid.

14 "The Privateers in New York," *New York Times*, July 23, 1861, 6.

15 "The Story of Wm. Tillman, the Steward," *New York Tribune*, July 22, 1861, 8.

16 "The Privateers in New York," *New York Times*, July 23, 1861, 6.

17 Ibid.

18 "Appearance of the S. J. Waring and the Cabins Where the Men Were Killed," *New York Herald*, July 22, 1861, 4.

19 For a discussion of the law of salvage as applied to the recapture of the *S. J. Waring*, see chapter 7. For the decision of the U.S. District Court in the salvage trial, see chapter 8.

20 *New York Sun*, July 23, 1861.

21 "The Privateers in New York," *New York Times*, July 23, 1861, 6.

22 "Additional Particulars from Our Special Reporter," *New York Herald*, July 22, 1861, 4.

23 "The Negro William Tillman," *New York Herald*, July 22, 1861, 5.

24 "Recaptured Prize by a Black Hero," *The Liberator*, August 2, 1861; "The War and Colored American Auxiliaries," *The Liberator*, September 6, 1861.

25 "A Black Hero," *Douglass' Monthly*, August, 1861, 499.

26 "Letter to the President from Gerrit Smith," *The Liberator*, September 13, 1861; "Letter to the President from Gerrit Smith," *Douglass' Monthly*, October 1861.

27 Davis, *The Problem of Slavery in the Age of Emancipation*, 256.

28 "British West India Emancipation," *The Liberator*, August 9, 1861.

29 Henig, "William Tillman: The Union's First Black Hero," 83.

30 "Retaking of one of the Vessels Captured by the *Jeff. Davis*," *Scientific American*, August 3, 1861, 66–67; "The Schooner 'S. J. Waring,' Recaptured from the Pirates by the Negro Wm. Tillman," *Harper's Weekly* 5, no. 240 (August 3, 1861): 485; "The Negro Steward, Tillman, Killing the Prize Captain of the S. J. Waring," *Frank Leslie's Illustrated Newspaper*, August 3, 1861, 192; "A Negro Cook Slays Three of His Captors," *Sacramento Union*, August 8, 1861.

31 Henig, "William Tillman: The Union's First Black Hero," 83.

32 "William Tillman: Phrenological Character and Biography," *American Phrenological Journal and Life Illustrated* 34, no. 3 (September 1861): 61–63.

33 McCandless, "Mesmerism and Phrenology in Antebellum Charleston: 'Enough of the Marvelous,'" 211.

34 Ibid., 212, 228.

35 "William Tillman: Phrenological Character and Biography," 61.

36 Ibid., 61–62.

37 Ibid., 62.

38 Burlingame, *Abraham Lincoln: A Life*, 177.

39 John A. Kasson in Rice, *Reminiscences of Abraham Lincoln*, 378.

40 The *New York Times* wrote of Ellsworth that "his death will be regarded as a martyrdom, and his name will be enrolled upon the list of our country's patriots." *New York Times*, May 25, 1861.

41 McPherson, *Battle Cry of Freedom*, 333–334; Symonds, *The Civil War at Sea*, 110.

42 McPherson, *Battle Cry of Freedom*, 342.

43 Scarborough, *Diary of Edmund Ruffin: The Years of Hope, April, 1861– June, 1863*, 96.

44 Horace Greeley to Abraham Lincoln, July 29, 1861. Abraham Lincoln Papers, Library of Congress.

45 McPherson, *Battle Cry of Freedom*, 347, states that about four hundred Confederates were killed and that 625 Union troops were killed or mortally wounded. He notes, however, that the numbers of Civil War casualties cannot be known with certitude. The estimated numbers here are generally given in other sources, e.g.: Faust, *Historical Times Illustrated Encyclopedia of the Civil War*, 92.

46 A Drummond light (also known as limelight or calcium light) is a type of brilliant lamp once used to illuminate outdoor areas and buildings and to provide inside stage lighting for theaters and music halls.

47 Barnum, *The Life of P. T. Barnum, Written by Himself*, 68–91 (lecture on "The Art of Money-Getting").

48 Ibid., 38; Kunhardt, Kunhardt, and Kunhardt, *P. T. Barnum: America's Greatest Showman*, 20–23.

49 Saxon, *P. T. Barnum: The Legend and the Man*, 77, 335–336; Kunhardt, Kunhardt, and Kunhardt, *P. T. Barnum: America's Greatest Showman*, 46.

50 Saxon, *P. T. Barnum: The Legend and the Man*, 84–85.

51 Barnum, *The Life of P. T. Barnum, Written by Himself*, 229.

52 "Barnum's American Museum," *New York Tribune*, February 27, 1849.

53 Barnum, *The Life of P. T. Barnum, Written by Himself*, 228; Saxon, *P. T. Barnum: The Legend and the Man*, 215–216.

54 "The Pirate Slayers at Barnum's Museum," *New York Times*, July 25, 1861.

55 *Brooklyn Daily Eagle*, July 25, 1861.

56 "Barnum's American Museum," *New York Herald*, July 25, 1861, 7.

57 "Personal," *Frank Leslie's Weekly*, July 27, 1861.

58 "Barnum's American Museum," *Frank Leslie's Illustrated Newspaper*, August 10, 1861, 194.

59 "Barnum's American Museum," *New York Herald*, July 28, 1861, 7.

60 Libel of William Tillman, William Stedding, and Donald McLeod, July 27, 1861, in *William Tillman and others v. The Schooner S. J. Waring, her tackle, apparel, furniture, and cargo*, U.S. District Court, Southern District, New York. See also chapter 7.

61 See Cook, *The Colossal P. T. Barnum Reader: Nothing Else Like It in the Universe*, 155–157, 177. A surviving copy of the lithograph is preserved in the collections of the New-York Historical Society.

62 "Barnum's American Museum," *New York Herald*, August 10, 1861, 7.

63 Barnum, *The Life of P. T. Barnum, Written by Himself*, 240.

64 For interesting comments about Tillman's appearances with Barnum, see Hughes, *Spectacles of Reform*, 21–23, 24, 37.

SEVEN: A MATTER OF COMPENSATION

1 "By 1860 New York was handling two-thirds of all the nation's imports and one-third of its exports. The combined imports of Boston, Philadelphia, and Baltimore were less than New York's imports of textiles alone.... In the value of its imports and exports, as well as in the volume of shipping which entered and cleared, New York not only stood an easy first among American ports; but in all the world only London and Liverpool exceeded it." Albion, *The Rise of the Port of New York*, 386.

2 Marvin, *Treatise on the Law of Wreck and Salvage*, 31.

3 U.S. Const., art. III, sec. 2.

4 1 Stat. 73, "An act to establish the judicial courts of the United States," Section 9, September 24, 1789.

5 Biographical Directory of Federal Judges, 1789–present, http://www .fjc.gov/servlet/nGetInfo?jid=2180&cid=999&ctype=na&instate=na.

6 Marvin, *Treatise on the Law of Wreck and Salvage*, 105; Garner, *Black's Law Dictionary*, 8th ed., 1867.

7 Marvin, *Treatise on the Law of Wreck and Salvage*, 41, 105–106

8 Ibid., 1–3.

9 "The Steward of the S. J. Waring," *New York Times*, July 24, 1861, 5.

10   Ibid.
11   Libel of William Tillman, William Stedding, and Donald McLeod, July 27, 1861, in *William Tillman and others v. The Schooner S. J. Waring, her tackle, apparel, furniture, and cargo,* U.S. District Court, Southern District, New York.
12   Ibid.
13   Ibid.
14   Libel of Bryce MacKinnon, August 2, 1861, ibid.
15   Order for Consolidation, August 9, 1861, ibid.
16   Claim of Ownership, August 6, 1861; Attachment, August 13, 1861; Order of Discharge from Custody, August 9, 1861, ibid.
17   Townsend Scudder lived from 1829 to 1874. At the time of his death he was recognized as the leading admiralty lawyer in the United States, and the courts adjourned in his memory. Local annals recorded that the Scudder family had settled at Northport in the town of Huntington, Long Island, as early as 1652. Ross, *A History of Long Island,* 3:106.
18   Answer of Claimants in *William Tillman and others v. The Schooner S. J. Waring, her tackle, apparel, furniture, and cargo,* U.S. District Court, Southern District, New York.
19   Marvin, *Treatise on the Law of Wreck and Salvage,* 157–171.
20   Answer of Claimants in *William Tillman and others v. The Schooner S. J. Waring, her tackle, apparel, furniture, and cargo,* U.S. District Court, Southern District, New York. The Answer was filed in court on August 23 but signed by Jonas Smith on August 21.
21   "Proclamation for the Observance of Neutrality in the American Civil War, May 13, 1861," Deák and Jessup, *A Collection of Neutrality Laws, Regulations and Treaties of Various Countries,* 1:161–162; Neff, *Justice in Blue and Gray,* 168.

EIGHT: PASSING JUDGMENT

1   See Symonds, *The Civil War at Sea,* 78–79.
2   *Trial of the Officers and Crew of the Privateer Savannah, on the Charge of Piracy, in the United States Circuit Court for the Southern District of New York. Hon. Judges Nelson and Shipman, Presiding,* vi–xii.
3   See 1 Stat. 112–117, "An Act for the Punishment of certain Crimes against the United States," April 30, 1790; 3 Stat. 510, "An Act to

protect the commerce of the United States, and punish the crime of piracy," March 3, 1819; 3 Stat. 600–601, "An Act to continue in force 'An act to protect the commerce of the United States, and punish the crime of piracy,' and also to make further provision for punishing the crime of piracy," May 15, 1820.

4   *Trial of the Officers and Crew of the Privateer Savannah, on the Charge of Piracy, in the United States Circuit Court for the Southern District of New York. Hon. Judges Nelson and Shipman, Presiding,* 1.

5   *Official Records of the Union and Confederate Navies in the War of the Rebellion,* series 2, vol. 1, 364.

6   *The Jeff Davis Piracy Cases: Full Report of the Trial of William Smith for Piracy, as One of the Crew of the Confederate Privateer, the Jeff Davis: Before Judges Grier and Cadwalader, in the Circuit Court of the United States, for the Eastern District of Pennsylvania, held at Philadelphia, in October, 1861,* 12, 17, 21, 54.

7   Ibid., 27.

8   Ibid., 7.

9   *Official Records of the Union and Confederate Navies,* series 2, vol. 3, 97–98; see discussion in Chapter 3.

10   *Trial of the Officers and Crew of the Privateer Savannah, on the Charge of Piracy, in the United States Circuit Court for the Southern District of New York. Hon. Judges Nelson and Shipman, Presiding,* 117–169; *The Jeff Davis Piracy Cases: Full Report of the Trial of William Smith for Piracy, as One of the Crew of the Confederate Privateer, the Jeff Davis: Before Judges Grier and Cadwalader, in the Circuit Court of the United States, for the Eastern District of Pennsylvania, held at Philadelphia, in October, 1861,* 55–83. An extensive analysis of the arguments in these cases, much beyond the scope of this book, is presented in Weitz, *The Confederacy on Trial,* 132–190.

11   *Dred Scott v. Sandford,* 19 How. (60 U.S.) 393, 469 (1857).

12   *The Jeff Davis Piracy Cases: Full Report of the Trial of William Smith for Piracy, as One of the Crew of the Confederate Privateer, the Jeff Davis: Before Judges Grier and Cadwalader, in the Circuit Court of the United States, for the Eastern District of Pennsylvania, held at Philadelphia, in October, 1861,* 46.

13   Ibid., 95–97.

14   Ibid., 97–99.

15   *Dred Scott v. Sandford,* 19 How. (60 U.S.) 393, 457–469 (1857).

16   *Trial of the Officers and Crew of the Privateer Savannah, on the Charge of Piracy, in the United States Circuit Court for the Southern District of New York. Hon. Judges Nelson and Shipman, Presiding*, 373–374; Weitz, *The Confederacy on Trial*, 189.

17   *The Jeff Davis Piracy Cases: Full Report of the Trial of William Smith for Piracy, as One of the Crew of the Confederate Privateer, the Jeff Davis: Before Judges Grier and Cadwalader, in the Circuit Court of the United States, for the Eastern District of Pennsylvania, held at Philadelphia, in October, 1861*, 99–100.

18   Jefferson Davis to Abraham Lincoln, July 6, 1861, *The War of the Rebellion: A Compilation of the Official Records of the Union and Confederate Armies*, series 2, vol. 3, 5–6; Neff, *Justice in Blue and Gray*, 64.

19   Neff, *Justice in Blue and Gray*, 24, 64; Weitz, *The Confederacy on Trial*, 195–196; Witt, *Lincoln's Code*, 162. Almost immediately after the conviction in Philadelphia, the Confederate War Department ordered that Union prisoners matching the numbers and ranks of the Northern convicts be selected for retaliatory executions. See Weitz, *The Confederacy on Trial*, 195.

20   Lincoln's government regarded its refusal to execute prisoners as a "humanitarian gesture, a matter of grace and free will on its own part," rather than a legal requirement. See Neff, *Justice in Blue and Gray*, 21.

21   Testimony of William Tillman, Minutes of Testimony, *William Tillman and others v. The Schooner S. J. Waring, her tackle, apparel, furniture, and cargo*, U.S. District Court, Southern District, New York.

22   Testimony of William Stedding, ibid.

23   Testimony of Bryce MacKinnon, ibid.

24   Ibid.

25   Ibid.

26   Testimony of Donald McLeod, ibid.

27   Points and Authorities. ibid.

28   "United States District Court Southern District of New York," *New York Times*, December 24, 1861.

29   Ibid.

30   Marvin, *Treatise on the Law of Wreck and Salvage*, 113–114n2, quoting from the case of *The Bark Dygden*, 1 Notes of Cases 115.

31 Marvin, *Treatise on the Law of Wreck and Salvage*, 114n2, quoting from the case of *Cape Packet*, 3 W. Rob. 122.

32 "United States District Court Southern District of New York," *New York Times*, December 24, 1861.

33 Ibid.

34 Ibid.

35 The Case of the Colored Steward William Tillman," *New York Times*, December 25, 1861.

36 Ibid.

37 Decree filed February 6, 1862, *William Tillman and others v. The Schooner S. J. Waring, her tackle, apparel, furniture, and cargo*, U.S. District Court, Southern District, New York.

NINE: THE FURY CONTINUES

1   Rowland, *Jefferson Davis, Constitutionalist: His Letters, Papers and Speeches*, 1:286; see Davis, *Jefferson Davis: The Man and His Hour*, 195; Oakes, *Freedom National: The Destruction of Slavery in the United States, 1861–1865*, 43–44.

2   Dew, *Apostles of Disunion*, 14–15.

3   Cleveland, *Alexander H. Stephens*, 721.

4   Basler, *Collected Works of Abraham Lincoln*, 2:461, 2:492, 3:18, 7:281; McPherson, *Battle Cry of Freedom*, 309–311 ; Oakes, *Freedom National: The Destruction of Slavery in the United States, 1861–1865*, 1–48.

5   Basler, *Collected Works of Abraham Lincoln*, 2:532.

6   Ibid., 1:75, 4:263, 4:160, 3:16.

7   Burlingame, *Abraham Lincoln: A Life*, 2:154–159; see Basler, *Collected Works of Abraham Lincoln*, 4:532.

8   According to William Wells Brown, author of the first assessment of African American contributions to the Civil War, the sympathies of blacks in both the North and the South were with the Union. He wrote as early as 1863: "At the North, they were among the earliest to respond to the president's first proclamation, calling for troops. At the south, they have ever shown a preference for the *stars and stripes*." Brown, *The Black Man*, 50.

9   See Washington, *Up from Slavery*, 7–8.

10 Hargrove, *Black Union Soldiers in the Civil War*, 2–3; McPherson, *The Negro's Civil War*, 19–21; Quarles, *The Negro in the Civil War*, 24–29.

11 1 Stat. 271, "An Act more effectually to provide for the National Defense by establishing an Uniform Militia throughout the United States," May 8, 1872.

12 Quarles, *The Negro in the Civil War*, 31.

13 Clark, *The Black Brigade of Cincinnati*, 4–5.

14 McPherson, *The Negro's Civil War*, 24–25.

15 12 Stat. 319, "An Act to confiscate Property used for Insurrectionary Purposes," August 6, 1861.

16 12 Stat. 376, "An act for the release of certain persons held to service or labor in the District of Columbia," April 16, 1862.

17 12 Stat. 589–592, "An act to suppress insurrection, to punish treason and rebellion, to seize and confiscate the property of rebels, and for other purposes," July 17, 1862.

18 Basler, *Collected Works of Abraham Lincoln*, 6:28–30.

19 12 Stat. 731–737, "An Act for enrolling and calling out the national Forces, and for other Purposes," March 3, 1863. Exceptions were provided for hardship cases (for example, the only son of a widowed mother) and for men who could either furnish substitutes or pay the sum of three hundred dollars. The enrollees were also divided into two classes. Class 1 included all single men and married men between the ages of twenty and thirty-five. Class 2 included men married over thirty-five. Men from Class 2 would not be drafted until Class 2 had been exhausted. See McPherson, *Battle Cry of Freedom*, 600–601n20.

20 Burrows and Wallace, *Gotham*, 895.

21 McPherson, *The Negro's Civil War*, 175.

22 "The Siege of Fort Wagner: Conduct of the Massachusetts Negro Regiment," *New York Times*, July 31, 1863.

23 "The Ovation to the Black Regiment," *New York Times*, March 7, 1864.

24 Varon, *Appomattox*, 94.

25 Douglass, "A Black Hero," 499.

26 Rouse, *The Bugle Blast; or Spirit of the Conflict*, 80–84.

27 *The Rebel Pirate's Fatal Prize; or, The Bloody Tragedy of the Prize Schooner Waring*, 17–18.

28 Brown, *The Negro in the American Rebellion: His Heroism and His Fidelity*, 74–75.

29 Washington, *A New Negro for a New Century*, 283–284.

30 *Consolidated Lists of Civil War Draft Registration Records (Provost Marshal General's Bureau; Consolidated Enrollment Lists, 1863–1865)*; Record Group: *110, Records of the Provost Marshal General's Bureau (Civil War)*; Collection Name: *Consolidated Enrollment Lists, 1863–1865 (Civil War Union Draft Records)*; National Archives and Records Administration. This entry lists the enrollee's birthplace as Pennsylvania. Since the hero of the *S. J. Waring* was born in Delaware, this raises a slight question as to the identity of the enrollee. It is not a substantial question, however, for the other elements of the listing are consistent with William Tillman. Further, it is well known that census takers and draft enumerators frequently made errors. For example, the draft registration for John D. Rockefeller, later renowned as the richest man in the United States, gave his name as "John W. Rockefeller," but researchers are convinced that the record was in fact for "John D. Rockefeller." See Michael T. Meier, "Civil War Draft Records: Exemptions and Enrollments," *Prologue Magazine* 26, no. 4 (Winter 1994), at http://www.archives.gov/publications/prologue/1994/winter/civil-war-draft-records.html.

31 Two able-bodied Northern men who did not see military service were the future president of the United States Grover Cleveland and the future billionaire John D. Rockefeller. See Michael T. Meier, "Civil War Draft Records: Exemptions and Enrollments," *Prologue Magazine* 26, no. 4 (Winter 1994), at http://www.archives.gov/publications/prologue/1994/winter/civil-war-draft-records.html.

32 See discussion in chapter 7.

33 *Rhode Island Marriages*, 1851–1920, online at Ancestry.com.

34 *Providence, Rhode Island, City Directory*, 1864, p. 149, online at Ancestry.com.

35 *Rhode Island State Census*, 1865–1935, online at Ancestry.com.

36 United States Census for 1870, Cranston, Providence, Rhode Island.

37 United States Census for 1880, San Francisco, California; San Francisco City Directory for 1880. Of course, these records must be read with caution and with the awareness that they might possibly be for another black cook named William Tillman. Under all the circum-

stances, however, it seems quite probable that they are for the subject of this book and not any other man. Like life itself, history is subject to uncertainties and vagaries that cannot be completely escaped.

38   Redd, *St. Augustine and the Civil War*, 49.

39   *Charleston Daily Mercury*, August 26, 1861; see Robinson, *The Confederate Privateers*, 78.

40   *Search for the* Jefferson Davis*: Trader, Slaver, Raider* (Glens Falls, NY: Pepe Productions; St. Augustine, FL: St. Augustine Lighthouse and Museum, 2011).

41   McPherson, *War on the Waters*, 21; see Robinson, *The Confederate Privateers*, 66 ("The cruise of the *Jefferson Davis* may be ranked as the last truly classic cruise in the history of private-armed sea power, worthy to stand with the most notable cruises of our letters of marque of 1776 and 1812").

42   McPherson, *War on the Waters*, 21.

43   See Robinson, *The Confederate Privateers*, 343 ("The institution of privateering was obsolete and no amount of industry and valor could save it. It belonged to a vanished order of things, like the very political and social structure which the Confederate States themselves typified").

44   Symonds, *The Civil War at Sea*, 79–80.

45   McPherson, *War on the Waters*, 22; Symonds, *The Civil War at Sea*, 79.

46   Testimony of Bryce MacKinnon in *William Tillman and others v. The Schooner S. J. Waring, her tackle, apparel, furniture, and cargo*, U.S. District Court, Southern District, New York.

47   Commander George A. Prentiss of U.S.S. *Albatross* to Flag-Officer Samuel F. Du Pont, Commanding the South Atlantic Blockading Squadron, July 3, 1862. *Official Records of the Union and Confederate Navies in the War of the Rebellion*, series 1, vol. 13, 124 (103 casks of rice). A prize proceeding followed. See "Letter from the Secretary of the Navy, in Answer to a Resolution of the House, of the 15th Instant, Relative to the Disposition of Prize Cases in New York." 38th Cong., 1st Sess.. House of Representatives. Ex. Doc. No. 74.

48   "The Sinking of the Steamship Evening Star," *Rochester Daily Union and Advertiser*, October 10, 1866; "Statement of Robert Finger, Chief Engineer," *Evening Courier and Republic* [Buffalo, New York], October 17, 1866.

49   "Industry Captains of Stony Brook," online at http://trees.ancestry

.com/tree/62611150/person/30093789510/photo/4da1079b–57ce–49aa
–bb51–8964bea77b99?src=search.

50   Recollections of Edward H. Davis, typewritten manuscript, p. 21, in
       Edward H. Davis Papers, San Diego Historical Society, San Diego,
       CA.

EPILOGUE

1   Henig, "The Union's First Black Hero: William Tillman," 84. Henig
       has suggested that relatives or friends of the Confederate privateers
       Tillman killed when recapturing the *S. J. Waring* may have been seek-
       ing revenge against him and that Tillman was trying to avoid them,
       although Henig admits that this is only speculation and that he has no
       evidence to support it. Henig to author, December 13, 2014.

2   Henig, "The Unstoppable Mr. Smalls," 43, points out that Smalls was
       designated as a "wheelman" because the title of "pilot" was not then
       permitted to black men. His duties and responsibilities were the same
       as those of a pilot.

3   *Official Records of the Union and Confederate Navies in the War of the
       Rebellion*, series 1, vol. 12, 807, 820–826; Miller, *Gullah Statesman:
       Robert Smalls from Slavery to Congress, 1839–1915*, 1–3; Billingsley,
       Yearning to Breathe Free, 51–65.

4   Letter of Flag-Officer Samuel F. Du Pont, May 22, 1862, in *Official
       Records of the Union and Confederate Navies in the War of the Rebellion*,
       series 7, vol. 12, 807.

5   *Congressional Globe*, 37th Cong., 2d sess., 1862, 2186–2187, 2363–
       2364, 2394, 2440; 12 Stat. 904, "An Act for the Benefit of Robert
       Small [*sic*], and others," May 30, 1862; *Official Records of the Union and
       Confederate Navies in the War of the Rebellion*, series 1, vol. 12, 823–826;
       Miller, *Gullah Statesman: Robert Smalls from Slavery to Congress, 1839–
       1915*, 11–12. Billingsley, *Yearning to Breathe Free*, contains at least two
       statements that Smalls was recognized as the "first hero" of the Civil
       War. On page 1 Billingsley states: "On the floor of the U.S. Congress,
       Smalls was declared 'the first hero of the Civil War.'" On page 61 Bill-
       ingsley states: "Newspapers and magazines all over the North hailed
       Smalls's feat, some declaring him the first hero of the war." Neither of
       these statements is supported by any note or other citation, and I have

been unable to discover any. Though Smalls was indeed a hero, the fact is that he was far from the "first hero" of the Civil War. William Tillman's recapture of the *S. J. Waring* on July 16, 1861, preceded Robert Smalls's capture of the *Planter* on May 13, 1862, by nearly eleven months, and other persons (for example, Elmer Ellsworth) may also have some claim to be recognized as "the first hero" of the Civil War.

6   Uya, *From Slavery to Public Service: Robert Smalls, 1839–1915*, 20–22; Henig, "The Unstoppable Mr. Smalls," 49.

7   See Miller, *Gullah Statesman: Robert Smalls from Slavery to Congress, 1839–1915*, 35–262; Henig, "The Unstoppable Mr. Smalls," 49.

8   U.S. Const., Amendment XIII, Sec. 1.

9   Ibid., Amendment XIV, Sec. 1.

10   *Dred Scott v. Sandford*, 19 How. (60 U.S.) 393 (1857).

11   U.S. Constitution, Amendment XV, Sec. 1.

12   13 Stat. 507, "An act to establish a bureau for the relief of freedmen and refugees," March 3, 1865.

13   14 Stat. 27, "An Act to protect all Persons in the United States in their Civil Rights, and furnish the Means for their Vindication," April 9, 1866.

14   Henig, "The Unstoppable Mr. Smalls," 49; see Clyburn, foreword to Billingsley, *Yearning to Breathe Free*, xii ("The South Carolina history books I grew up with contained no mention, not even in footnotes, of Robert Smalls and his extraordinary contributions to our state's history"); Miller, *Gullah Statesman: Robert Smalls from Slavery to Congress, 1839–1915*, x (Smalls "probably would have been more prominent in the memory of South Carolinians and in the South had not the post–Civil War society he helped to create been destroyed by the tide of reactionary forces").

15   Bierce, *Collected Works*, 7:138.

16   Turner, "The Significance of History," 180.

17   Hubbard, *The Roycroft Dictionary*, 69.

BIBLIOGRAPHY

Abraham Lincoln Papers. Library of Congress, Washington, DC.

Albion, Robert Greenhalgh. *The Rise of the Port of New York, 1815–1860.* New York: Charles Scribner's Sons, 1939.

American Lloyd's Registry of American and Foreign Shipping, Established in 1857. New York: E. and G. W. Blunt, 1859.

Ayers, Edward L. *What Caused the Civil War? Reflections on the South and Southern History.* New York: W. W. Norton, 2005.

Barnum, P. T. *The Humbugs of the World: An Account of Humbugs, Delusions, Impositions, Quackeries, Deceits, and Deceivers Generally, in All Ages.* New York: Carleton, 1866.

———. *The Life of P. T. Barnum, Written by Himself.* Buffalo, NY: Courier Company, 1888.

Basler, Roy P. *The Collected Works of Abraham Lincoln.* 8 vols. New Brunswick, NJ: Rutgers University Press, 1953.

Bayles, Richard M. *Historical and Descriptive Sketches of Suffolk County and Its Towns, Villages, Hamlets, Scenery, Institutions and Important Enterprises.* Port Jefferson, NY: The Author, 1874.

Beard, Rick. "'The Lion of the Day.'" New York Times Opinionator, August 4, 2011. http://opinionator.blogs.nytimes.com/2011/08/04/the-lion-of-the-day/?_php=true&_type=blogs&_r=0.

Bierce, Ambrose. *The Collected Works of Ambrose Bierce.* 7 vols. New York and Washington, DC: Neale Publishing Co., 1906.

Billingsley, Andrew. *Yearning to Breathe Free: Robert Smalls of South Carolina and His Families.* Columbia: University of South Carolina Press, 2007.

Blunt, Edmund M. *The American Coast Pilot; containing Directions for the*

Principal Harbors, Capes and Headlands of the Coasts of North and South America. 18th ed. New York: Edmund and George W. Blunt, 1857.

Bolster, W. Jeffrey. *Black Jacks: African American Seamen in the Age of Sail.* Cambridge, MA: Harvard University Press, 1997.

Botkin, B. A. *A Civil War Treasury of Tales, Legends, and Folklore.* New York: Random House, 1960.

Brown, William Wells. *The Black Man: His Antecedents, His Genius, and His Achievements.* New York: Thomas Hamilton/Boston, R. F. Wallcut, 1863.

———. *The Negro in the American Rebellion: His Heroism and His Fidelity.* Boston: A. G. Brown & Co., 1880. Reprint, Miami, FL: Mnemosyne Publishing, 1969.

Burlingame, Michael. *Abraham Lincoln: A Life.* 2 vols. Baltimore: Johns Hopkins University Press, 2008.

Burrows, Edwin G., and Mike Wallace. *Gotham: A History of New York City to 1898.* New York: Oxford University Press, 1999.

Carola, Chris. "The Civil War's First Black Hero." My Hero Project. http://www.myhero.com/myhero/go/specialevents/hero.asp?hero=civil_war_black_hero_2011_AP&eid=1.

Chidsey, Donald Barr. *The American Privateers.* New York: Dodd, Mead, 1962.

Clark, Peter H. *The Black Brigade of Cincinnati: Being a Report of its Labors and a Muster-roll of its Members, Together with Various Orders, Speeches, etc., relating to it.* Cincinnati: Joseph T. Boyd, 1864.

Cleveland, Henry. *Alexander H. Stephens, in Public and Private, with Letters and Speeches, Before, During, and Since the War.* Philadelphia: National Publishing Co., 1866.

Clyburn, James E. Foreword to Andrew Billingsley, *Yearning to Breathe Free: Robert Smalls of South Carolina and His Families.* Columbia: University of South Carolina Press, 2007.

Conventions and Declarations between the Powers Concerning War, Arbitration and Neutrality. The Hague: Martinus Nijhoff, 1915.

Cook, James W., ed. *The Colossal P. T. Barnum Reader: Nothing Else Like It in the Universe.* Urbana and Chicago: University of Illinois Press, 2005.

Cosgrove, John N. *Gray Days and Gold: A Character Sketch of Atlantic Mutual Insurance Company.* N.p.: Privately printed for the Atlantic Companies, 1967.

Cottrol, Robert J. *The Afro-Yankees: Providence's Black Community in the Antebellum Era.* Westport, CT: Greenwood Press, 1982.

Cutler, Carl C. *Queens of the Western Ocean: The Story of America's Mail and Passenger Sailing Lines.* Annapolis, MD: U.S. Naval Institute, 1961.

Dana, Richard Henry, Jr. *The Seaman's Friend: Containing a Treatise on Practical Seamanship.* 14th rev. ed. Boston: Thomas Groom, 1879. Reprint: Mineola, NY: Dover Publications, 1997.

———. *Two Years Before the Mast: A Personal Narrative of Life at Sea.* Edited by John Haskell Kemble. 2 vols. Los Angeles: Ward Ritchie Press, 1964. Originally published (anonymously) in New York by Harper & Brothers, 1840.

Davis, David Brion. *Inhuman Bondage: The Rise and Fall of Slavery in the New World.* New York: Oxford University Press, 2006.

———. *The Problem of Slavery in the Age of Emancipation.* New York: Alfred A. Knopf, 2014.

Davis, Edward H. Handwritten manuscripts and typescripts. San Diego Historical Society, San Diego, CA.

Davis, William C. *Battle at Bull Run: A History of the First Major Campaign of the Civil War.* Mechanicsburg, PA: Stackpole Books, 1995.

———. *Jefferson Davis: The Man and His Hour.* New York: HarperCollins, 1991.

Deák, Francis, and Philip C. Jessup. *A Collection of Neutrality Laws, Regulations and Treaties of Various Countries.* Vol. 1. Washington, DC: Carnegie Endowment for International Peace, 1939.

Dew, Charles B. *Apostles of Disunion: Southern Secession Commissioners and the Causes of the Civil War.* Charlottesville and London: University of Virginia Press, 2001.

Douglass, Frederick. "'A Black Hero,' *Douglass' Monthly.* August 1861." In *Frederick Douglass, the Heroic Slave: A Cultural and Critical Edition.* Edited by Robert S. Levine, John Stauffer, and John R. McKivigan, 138–142. New Haven/London: Yale University Press, 2015.

Essah, Patience. *A House Divided: Slavery and Emancipation in Delaware, 1638–1865.* Charlottesville: University Press of Virginia, 1996.

Farr, James Baker. *Black Odyssey: The Seafaring Traditions of Afro-Americans.* New York: Peter Lang, 1989.

Faust, Patricia L., ed. *Historical Times Illustrated Encyclopedia of the Civil War.* New York: Harper & Row, 1986.

Fehrenbacher, Don E. *The Slaveholding Republic: An Account of the United States Government's Relations to Slavery.* Completed and edited by Ward M. McAfee. New York: Oxford University Press, 2001.

Garner, Bryan A. *Black's Law Dictionary.* 8th ed. St. Paul, MN: Thomson West, 2006.

Gates, Henry Louis. "Who Was the First African American?" http://www .theroot.com/articles/history/2012/10/who_was_the_first_african_ american_100_amazing_facts_about_the_negro.html.

Gibbs, C. R. "A Story of High Seas Heroism: The Story of William Tillman." U.S. Department of Transportation, Maritime Administration. http://www.marad.dot.gov/education_landing_page/k_12/k_12_ salute/k12_william_tillman/william_tillman_detail_page.htm.

Gibson, Campbell, and Kay Jung. "Historical Census Statistics on Population Totals by Race, 1790 to 1990, and by Hispanic Origin, 1970 to 1990, for the United States, Regions, Divisions, and States." Working Paper Series No. 56. Population Division, U. S. Census Bureau, Washington, DC 20233. September 2002. http://www.census.gov/ population/www/documentation/twps0056/twps0056.html.

Fiske, David, Clifford W. Brown, and Rachel Seligman. *Solomon Northup: The Complete Story of the Author of* Twelve Years a Slave. Santa Barbara, CA: Praeger, 2013.

Fowler, William M., Jr. *Under Two Flags: The American Navy in the Civil War.* New York: W. W. Norton, 1990.

Hamilton, Cynthia S. "Models of Agency: Frederick Douglass and 'The Heroic Slave.'" *Proceedings of the American Antiquarian Society* 114, part 1 (April 2004): 87–136.

Hancock, Harold B. *The History of Sussex County, Delaware.* N.p.: Privately printed, 1976.

———. "Not Quite Men: The Free Negroes in Delaware in the 1830's." *Civil War History* 17 (1971): 320–331.

———. "William Yates's Letter of 1837: Slavery and Colored People in Delaware." *Delaware History* 14 (1971): 205–216.

Hargrove, Hondon B. *Black Union Soldiers in the Civil War.* Jefferson, NC: McFarland, 1988.

Heathcote, T. A. *The British Admirals of the Fleet, 1734–1991: A Biographical Dictionary.* Barnsley, South Yorkshire, UK: Pen and Sword Books, 2002.

Henig, Gerald S. "The Unstoppable Mr. Smalls." *America's Civil War* 20, no. 1 (March, 2007): 40–49.

———. "William Tillman: The Union's First Black Hero." *North & South* 10, no. 2 (July 2007): 80–85.

History of Suffolk County, New York, with Illustrations, Portraits, and Sketches of Prominent Families and Individuals. New York: W.W. Munsell, 1882.

Hubbard, Elbert. *The Roycroft Dictionary Concocted by Ali Baba and the Bunch on Rainy Days.* [East Aurora, NY]: The Roycrofters, 1914.

Hughes, Amy E. *Spectacles of Reform: Theater and Activism in Nineteenth-Century America.* Ann Arbor: University of Michigan Press, 2012.

Hunter, Tera W. "Putting an Antebellum Myth to Rest." *New York Times,* August 1, 2011.

The Jeff Davis Piracy Cases: Full Report of the Trial of William Smith for Piracy, as One of the Crew of the Confederate Privateer, the Jeff Davis: Before Judges Grier and Cadwalader, in the Circuit Court of the United States, for the Eastern District of Pennsylvania, held at Philadelphia, in October, 1861. By D. F. Murphy. Philadelphia: King & Baird, Printers, 1861.

"Jefferson Davis." *Dictionary of American Naval Fighting Ships.* Department of the Navy, Naval History and Heritage Command. http://www .history.navy.mil/danfs/cfa5/jefferson_davis.htm.

Jones, Steven W. "A Confederate Prize Crew Meets Its Match in William Tillman." *Sea History* 93 (Summer 2000): 34–36.

Klein, Howard. *Three Village Guidebook: The Setaukets, Poquott, Old Field & Stony Brook.* 2nd ed. East Setauket, NY: Three Village Historical Society, 1986.

Kunhardt, Philip B., Jr., Philip B. Kunhardt III, and Peter W. Kunhardt. *P. T. Barnum: America's Greatest Showman.* New York: Alfred A. Knopf, 1995.

Litwack, Leon F. *North of Slavery: The Negro in the Free States, 1790–1860.* Chicago: University of Chicago Press, 1961.

Lubet, Steven. *Fugitive Justice: Runaways, Rescuers, and Slavery on Trial.* Cambridge, MA: Belknap Press of Harvard University Press, 2010.

Mackay, Charles. *Life and Liberty in America; or, Sketches of a Tour in the United States and Canada in 1857–8.* New York: Harper & Brothers, 1859.

Marvin, William. *A Treatise on the Law of Wreck and Salvage.* Boston: Little, Brown, 1858.

McCandless, Peter. "Mesmerism and Phrenology in Antebellum Charleston: 'Enough of the Marvellous.'" *Journal of Southern History* 58 (1992): 199–230.

McGinty, Brian. *The Body of John Merryman: Abraham Lincoln and the Suspension of Habeas Corpus.* Cambridge, MA: Harvard University Press, 2011.

———. *Lincoln and the Court.* Cambridge, MA: Harvard University Press, 2008.

McPherson, James M. *Battle Cry of Freedom: The Civil War Era.* New York: Oxford University Press, 1988.

———. *The Negro's Civil War: How American Blacks Felt and Acted During the War for the Union.* New York: Ballantine Books, 1991.

———. *This Mighty Scourge: Perspectives on the Civil War.* New York: Oxford University Press, 2007.

———. *War on the Waters: The Union and Confederate Navies, 1861–1865.* Chapel Hill: University of North Carolina Press, 2012.

Miller, Edward A., Jr. *Gullah Statesman: Robert Smalls from Slavery to Congress, 1839–1915.* Columbia: University of South Carolina Press, 1995.

Neff, Stephen C. *Justice in Blue and Gray: A Legal History of the Civil War.* Cambridge, MA: Harvard University Press, 2010.

"The Negro Steward, Tillman, Killing the Prize Captain of the S. J. Waring." *Frank Leslie's Illustrated Newspaper,* August 3, 1861, 192.

Newton, James E. "Black Americans in Delaware: An Overview." http://www.udel.edu/BlackHistory/overview.html.

New-York Marine Register: A Standard of Classification of American Vessels, and of Such Other Vessels as Visit American Ports. New York: R. C. Root, Anthony & Co., Printers to the Board of Underwriters, 1857.

Northup, Solomon. *Twelve Years a Slave.* Introduction by Ira Berlin. Henry Louis Gates, Jr., general ed. New York: Penguin Books, 2008.

"Notes on the Coast of the United States by A .B. Bache, Sup'dt U.S. Survey. Section V. Coast of South Carolina (with 8 maps). June 1861." National Oceanic and Atmospheric Administration (NOAA). http://www.nauticalcharts.noaa.gov/nsd/hcp_notesoncoast.html.

Official Records of the Union and Confederate Navies in the War of the Rebellion. 30 vols. Washington, DC: Government Printing Office, 1894–1922.

Petrie, Donald A. *The Prize Game: Lawful Looting on the High Seas in the Days of Fighting Sail.* New York: Berkley Books, 1999.

Poser, Susan, and Elizabeth R. Varon. "United States v. Steinmetz: The Legal Legacy of the Civil War, Revisited." *Alabama Law Review* 46 (1995): 725–762.

Quarles, Benjamin. *The Negro in the Civil War.* Boston: Little, Brown, 1953. Reprint: New York, Da Capo, 1989.

Randall, James G. *Constitutional Problems under Lincoln.* Rev. ed. Urbana: University of Illinois Press, 1964.

The Rebel Pirate's Fatal Prize; or, the Bloody Tragedy of the Prize Schooner Waring, Enacted As the Rebels Were Attempting To Run Her Into Charleston, S.C., July 7, 1861; Being the Life and Confessions of the Steward, William Tillman, the Brave and Daring Negro, Who, With a Hatchet, Murdered the Rebel Prize Master, Lieutenant, and Mate, Whom He Overheard Secretly Plotting to Sell Him into Slavery, Recaptured the Vessel, and Brought Her into a Free Port; also the Thrilling History of Hope Carter, the Mulatto Contraband and Tennessee Slave; Together with the Sinking of the Rebel Privateer, Petrel, by the U.S. Frigate, St. Lawrence, the Capture of "Jeff. Davis" and the Enchantress, and Trial of the Rebel Pirates. By a Passenger of the Waring and an Eye Witness to the Bloody Scenes. Philadelphia: Barclay and Co., 1865.

Redd, Robert. *St. Augustine and the Civil War.* Charleston, SC: History Press, 2014.

Reis, Benjamin. *The Showman and the Slave: Race, Death, and Memory in Barnum's America.* Cambridge, MA: Harvard University Press, 2010.

Report of the Officers Constituting the Light-House Board. 32nd Cong., 1st Sess. Ex. Doc. No. 28. Washington, DC: A. Boyd Hamilton, 1852.

"Retaking of one of the Vessels Captured by the *Jeff. Davis*." *Scientific American*, August 3, 1861, 66–67.

Rice, Allen Thorndike, ed. *Reminiscences of Abraham Lincoln by Distinguished Men of His Time.* New York: North American Review, 1888.

Robinson, William Morrison, Jr. *The Confederate Privateers.* New Haven: Yale University Press, 1928. Reprint, Columbia: University of South Carolina Press, 1990.

Ross, Peter. *A History of Long Island from Its Earliest Settlement to the Present Time.* Vol. 3. New York and Chicago: Lewis Publishing Co., 1903.

Rouse, E. S. S. *The Bugle Blast, or, The Spirit of the Conflict, Comprising Naval and Military Exploits, Dashing Raids, Heroic Deeds, Thrilling Incidents, Sketches, Anecdotes, etc., etc.* Philadelphia: James Challen and Son, 1864.

Rowland, Dunbar. *Jefferson Davis, Constitutionalist: His Letters, Papers and Speeches*. Vol. 1. Jackson, MS: Department of Archives and History, 1923.

Santayana, George. *The Life of Reason, or the Phases of Human Progress: Introduction and Reason in Common Sense*. London: Archibald Constable, 1906.

Saxon, A. H. *P. T. Barnum: The Legend and the Man*. New York: Columbia University Press, 1989.

Scarborough, William Kauffman, ed. *Diary of Edmund Ruffin: The Years of Hope, April, 1861–June, 1863*. Baton Rouge: Louisiana State University Press, 1976.

Scharf, J. Thomas. *History of the Confederate States Navy*. New York: Rogers and Sherwood, 1887.

"The Schooner 'S. J. Waring,' Recaptured from the Pirates by the Negro Wm. Tillman." *Harper's Weekly* 5, no. 240 (August 3, 1861): 485.

Sluby, Paul E., Sr., and Stanton L. Wormley, eds. Narrative of Billy Tilghman. Washington, DC: Columbian Harmony Society, 1983.

Soodalter, Ron. "The Short Life of a Rebel Privateer." New York Times Opinionator, August 17, 2011. http://opinionator.blogs.nytimes.com/2011/08/17/the-short-life-of-a-rebel-privateer/?_r=0.

Spann, Edward K. *Gotham at War: New York City, 1860–1865*. Wilmington, DE: SR Books, 2002.

Spears, John R. *The History of Our Navy from Its Origins to the End of the War with Spain*. Vol. 4. New York: Charles Scribner's Sons, 1899.

Stephens, Alexander H. *A Constitutional View of the Late War Between the States*. 2 vols. Philadelphia: National Publishing Co., 1870.

Sterling, Dorothy, ed. *Speak Out in Thunder Tones: Letters and Other Writings by Black Northerners, 1787–1865*. New York: Da Capo Press, 1998.

Symonds, Craig L. *The Civil War at Sea*. Santa Barbara, CA, and New York: Oxford University Press, 2012.

Three Village Historical Society. *The Images of America: Stony Brook*. Charleston, SC: Arcadia Publishing, 2003.

Tomes, Robert. *The War with the South: A History of the Late Rebellion*. Vol. 1. New York: Virtue and Yorston, 1862.

Trial of the Officers and Crew of the Privateer Savannah, on the Charge of Piracy, in the United States Circuit Court for the Southern District of

New York. Hon. Judges Nelson and Shipman, Presiding. Reported by A. F. Warburton, Stenographer, and corrected by the Counsel. New York: Baker & Godwin, 1862.

Turner, Frederick Jackson. "The Significance of History." In Stephen Vaughn, ed., *The Vital Past: Writings on the Uses of History*, 177–188. Athens: University of Georgia Press, 1955.

Turner, Sam. "The Search for the Jefferson Davis in the National Archives." 2007. http://www.staugustinelighthouse.org/LAMP/Historical_Re search/the-search-for-the-jefferson-davis.

U.S. Congress, *Congressional Globe*, 46 vols. Washington, DC, 1834–73.

Uya, Okon Edet. *From Slavery to Public Service: Robert Smalls 1839–1915.* New York: Oxford University Press, 1971.

Varon, Elizabeth R. *Appomattox: Victory, Defeat, and Freedom at the End of the Civil War.* New York: Oxford University Press, 2014.

Washington, Booker T. *A New Negro for a New Century: An Accurate and Up-to-Date Record of the Upward Struggle of the Negro Race.* Chicago: American Publishing House, 1900.

———. *Up From Slavery: An Autobiography.* New York: Doubleday, Page, 1901.

Weitz, Mark A. *The Confederacy on Trial: The Piracy and Sequestration Cases of 1861.* Lawrence: University Press of Kansas, 2005.

Welch, Richard F. *An Island's Trade: Nineteenth-Century Shipbuilding on Long Island.* Mystic, CT: Mystic Seaport Museum, 1993.

Wells, Carol. "William Ross Postell, Adventurer." *Georgia Historical Quarterly* 57 (1973): 390–405.

William Tillman and others v. The Schooner S. J. Waring, her tackle, apparel, furniture, and cargo. United States District Court for the Southern District of New York. Record Group 21, Records of the District Courts of the United States, Admiralty Case Files, 1790–1966. National Archives Identifier: 579537. Case A16–369. Records scanned at the National Archives at Kansas City, KS.

"William Tillman: Phrenological Character and Biography." *American Phrenological Journal and Life Illustrated, a Repository of Science, Literature, General Intelligence* 34, no. 31 (September 1861): 61–63.

Williams, William H. *Slavery and Freedom in Delaware, 1639–1865.* Wilmington, DE: Scholarly Resources, 1996.

Wilson, Carol. *Freedom at Risk: The Kidnapping of Free Blacks in America, 1780–1865.* Lexington: University Press of Kentucky, 1994.

Wise, Stephen R. *Lifeline of the Confederacy: Blockade Running During the Civil War.* Columbia: University of South Carolina Press, 1988.

Witt, John Fabian. *Lincoln's Code: The Laws of War in American History.* New York: Free Press, 2012.

ILLUSTRATION CREDITS

1. Photography ©New-York Historical Society.
2. Brian McGinty Collection.
3. Collection of Three Village Historical Society, NY.
4. Brian McGinty Collection.
5. Brian McGinty Collection.
6. Brian McGinty Collection.
7. Brian McGinty Collection.
8. Brian McGinty Collection.
9. Brian McGinty Collection.
10. Brian McGinty Collection.
11. Brian McGinty Collection.
12. Brian McGinty Collection.
13. Brian McGinty Collection.
14. Brian McGinty Collection.
15. Brian McGinty Collection.

INDEX

FREEPORT MEMORIAL LIBRARY